An Honest account of my Spiritual Journey and Afterlife Research

FINDING HOPE
IN THE
AFTERLIFE

JOSHUA LOUIS

21 Photographs & 36 Videos containing Evidence

www.HOPEparanormal.com

BALBOA.PRESS
A DIVISION OF HAY HOUSE

Balboa Press books may be ordered through booksellers or by contacting:

Balboa Press
A Division of Hay House
1663 Liberty Drive
Bloomington, IN 47403
www.balboapress.com
844-682-1282

Because of the dynamic nature of the Internet, any web addresses or links contained in this book may have changed since publication and may no longer be valid. The views expressed in this work are solely those of the author and do not necessarily reflect the views of the publisher, and the publisher hereby disclaims any responsibility for them.

The author of this book does not dispense medical advice or prescribe the use of any technique as a form of treatment for physical, emotional, or medical problems without the advice of a physician, either directly or indirectly. The intent of the author is only to offer information of a general nature to help you in your quest for emotional and spiritual well-being. In the event you use any of the information in this book for yourself, which is your constitutional right, the author and the publisher assume no responsibility for your actions.

Print information available on the last page.

ISBN: 978-1-9822-6256-3 (sc)
ISBN: 978-1-9822-6258-7 (hc)
ISBN: 978-1-9822-6257-0 (e)

Library of Congress Control Number: 2021901367

Balboa Press rev. date: 02/04/2021

This book is dedicated to the Big J., the Guides, and all of the H.O.P.E. followers

CONTENTS

PLEASE READ FIRST

Why I wrote this book and my vow to the reader.

THIS BOOK IS BASED ON my personal experiences and research in the metaphysical, paranormal, and instrumental-trans communication fields. Even though I have my own beliefs and will express them throughout this book, I have mostly included facts based on my research. I even have a chapter dedicated to differentiating facts from beliefs. When people's beliefs are challenged, they tend to shut out any further information on the subject—contrary to prior investigation. It's taken me a long time to accept some of these findings myself.

Throughout this book, there are footnotes, photographic evidence, and 36 suggested videos to watch on my YouTube channel. Many of the stories I share with you have a recommended video that contains the evidence I discuss.

My vow to you, the reader, is that everything that you read as my testimony, or see as evidence is all true and 100% real. You might ask why I would feel the need to tell you this. Because there are plenty of people out there that have embellished or faked evidence for monetary gain through exposure and notoriety. I also have a chapter dedicated to that as well. I started afterlife research because I couldn't believe other people's claims, and I certainly couldn't believe anything I saw on TV. All of this started because I was somewhat skeptical.

I wrote this book because it was a way to share all that I've learned throughout the years. Even though I have a channel where all of my work is displayed (YouTube.com/

HopeParanormalWhiteLight), when a person writes, they can share a much more in-depth experience, in my opinion. So I will hold nothing back. I will tell you the real deal, the nitty-gritty, the good, the bad, and everything in between.

Whether you are a scientific mind looking to analyze what I share with you, or a true spiritual seeker, know that I will share this work with anyone who's interested. We all have a right to know these things, to explore the unknown, and find out what's on the "Other side." The truth is, one day, we're all going to find out whether we like it or not.

I've read so many books on the afterlife, metaphysics, and spirituality. Even though I consider myself to be a reasonably intelligent individual, some authors write in ways a simple guy like myself can barely understand. You won't have that problem with this book. I'm not an expert, nor do I claim to be. What I am, is someone who has immersed himself in finding the truth about what happens to us when we die and how that information can help us while we're still here. Based on the findings, I'm also someone who believes that we have a direct impact on the spirit realm and that it has a major impact on us.

So, take that proverbial trip with me down the rabbit hole and allow me to show you what I have found over the last eight years of doing this research.

"We can easily forgive a child who is afraid of the dark; the real tragedy of life is when men are afraid of the Light."

–Plato

A TROUBLED PAST

AT ONE POINT IN LIFE, being a bottomed-out drug addict, facing life in prison, who wanted nothing more than to die, I would be the last guy you'd expect to be doing what I do today. If you'd told me 15 years ago that I'd become a psychic medium, able to talk with the dead and capture them speaking through voice recorders and spirit boxes, I would've certainly said you were insane.

I feel it's important that I share some of my past as it's a big part of why I do the work I do. Some people spend their lives trying to get away from their troubled past, only to relive it in the deep recesses of their subconscious. It was important when I started this journey of *"Spirit and Science"* that I didn't regret my past, but saw how my painful experiences could help others. When someone does this type of research and finds out the answers, many have now found out through doing it, that person's way of thinking changes. Based on whom I thought I was and how I lived my life, it still blows my mind when I look at where I am today.

My Early Years...
Growing up in Connecticut, I had a fairly normal life. I lived on a cul-de-sac, played with the neighborhood kids, and knew to come home when the street lights came on at dusk. My mother, a stay-at-home mom, always made sure we had clean clothes, hot meals, and plenty of activities to keep my younger sister and me busy. My dad, a job recruiter, taught me good morals and how to be a die-hard Yankee fan. Go Yanks! I was raised Catholic, and attending church on Sundays was a must. I eventually started attending Catholic school and became an altar boy. I found

early on that even though I had friends, I never really felt like I belonged. I was a very sensitive kid, too sensitive, some would say. I always felt bad for the underdog, and being that I was one of the smallest in my class, I was regularly picked on. My parents took me to karate, but I found it very ineffective for someone trying to defend themselves in real-life fighting situations. In schoolyards and the streets, anything goes, and I found the kids beating me up didn't want to wait for me to perfect my fighting techniques before pummeling me. Getting my ass handed to me on a regular basis, I knew my sensitivity was going to be my downfall. So, it became my mission to get rid of this glaring weakness.

Feeling isolated often, I would spend time riding my bike around town by myself. I'd sit in random churches when there was no one there, something most nine- and ten-year-olds didn't do. I'd sit and just stare at Jesus on the cross behind the altar, hoping He would move, maybe even wink at me. Weird, I know, but I always felt this connection to Jesus, a man I knew nothing about.

Fast forward to about age thirteen, that major flaw in my character, sensitivity, continued to rear its ugly head. I knew if I was ever going to survive this cruel and cold world, I needed to get rid of that weak part of me. The part that when seeing a small animal being hurt by boys my age made me want to step in and save it. The part that wanted to comfort a new kid in school because I knew what that felt like. Yes, if I were to make it, it would be because people respected me, even feared me, if it had to come to that. That meant hanging with the wrong kids and doing things no one else would do. This would prove to the world that I wasn't afraid when, in reality, that's all I was. A small group of us called ourselves a gang, and we beat up other kids and got in trouble.

Moved to Florida...

Eventually, my parents didn't know what to do with me and four schools later, being expelled from one of them, my father decided to move the family to South Florida. For him, the cost of living was much cheaper, and it would mean a new start for me. Problem was, along with a new place to live, a new school, new kids, there I still was—the same troublemaking punk from up North. In the first semester in ninth grade, I wanted to do right by my parents and missed the honor roll by only one grade. After that, I said forget it; I gave up. Before it was too late and the other kids found out who I really was, I went back to what I knew, being a juvenile delinquent. I found the troublemakers, and with that came the punishments, suspensions, and arrests. I stole cars, sold drugs, and didn't care about anyone unless they had a way to help me get what I wanted—respect. Being kicked out of my home on a weekly basis, my parents just couldn't control me.

By age eighteen, I had seen another four schools, ten misdemeanor arrests, and received a reputation for being nothing but trouble. Somehow I managed to receive a GED but found it was useless in getting a job. Not to mention, I was drinking every day before noon and had a dime-a-day cocaine habit from selling it. At this point, my high-school sweetheart was done with me, parents sickened by my behavior, and I had nothing left to do but become a full-fledged alcoholic and addict by nineteen. Now, it was at this moment in my life that something pivotal happened. I understood the significance then, but it wasn't until much later in my journey that I'd truly comprehend the gravity of what had happened late one night.

FIRST SPIRITUAL EXPERIENCE

I was at rock bottom, and I had never felt this low in my life. Having very little money allocated as the budget, my parents told me one night I was to go to rehab or I needed to get out. I was on the ropes and knew I had to take this offer; the pain was unbearable. I didn't even want to live anymore, but I was too scared to die, and I had no one left to turn to. Everyone was sick of me. I was even sick of me. It was late, around two in the morning, and I decided to go for a drive. I had absolutely nowhere to go but couldn't sit in my room any longer. It began to feel like a jail cell. With everyone asleep, I got into my beat-up Chrysler Sebring that had started to resemble a demolition car from the abuse over the years and drove it aimlessly around town. Driving down the main road with absolutely no one on it, I came upon a church and decided to pull in. I saw it was closed and even looked over at the rectory, hoping to see a priest, but all the lights were off. To the side of the church was a small grotto that housed a statue of the Virgin Mary holding the baby Jesus along with a small stand holding a few lit candles. In front of that, two short pews for kneeling and praying. I found a parking spot in the empty lot and walked into the grotto and over to the statue.

Just like when I was nine, I stared at the statue with childlike faith that maybe Mary would move, but she didn't. I put a dollar in the lockbox, lit a candle, and kneeled at one of the pews. I remember crying uncontrollably, sobbing to God about all I had done. The stealing, the cheating, the lying, and all the loved ones I had hurt. At that point, I didn't know what else to do. The pain was so intense, and something had to change. I prayed for forgiveness, and in my prayers, with hands clenched, I asked for a person that I could speak with, someone to confess my sins to. I was being honest with myself and God at that moment for the first time in my life it felt like, but I still needed to share it with someone else. As quickly as I asked for this, a little older lady holding a small dog walked into the grotto at two two-thirty in the morning. I couldn't believe my eyes and wiped the tears and snot away before she'd notice. Holding her dog, she whispered what seemed like prayers as she made her way over to the candles. As she lit one, something came over me. I remember feeling compassion, and I immediately prayed for the woman and her dog, thinking maybe the dog was sick. What I'm about to share with you is so crazy; I've had to sit and fully recount the whole experience many times because of how unbelievable it is.

This small woman walked over from the candles and kneeled in the pew next to me. At this point, I was fully able to contain my crying and just kneeled there with my head down. I then felt a gentle touch on my shoulder, and a soft voice say, "Would you like to confess your sins to me?" I looked up at this woman and just immediately burst out crying even harder than I was before if that was even possible. With tears once again falling down my face and snot running from my nose, I looked at this kind rosy-faced woman with brown eyes and a loving smile and said, "Yes, oh thank you, thank you." The woman pulled out an old, small book and, just like a priest, began giving me a confession. "Bless me, for it has been years since my last confession," I meekly spoke. I then went on to tell her all the horrible things I had done to friends, family, strangers, and myself.

Once I was done, she gave me my penance, prayers for me to say on my own, and then we prayed together. At that moment, I felt a great weight lifted from me. She then said, "Hold on, I have something I'd like to give you." I told her I couldn't accept anything more from her, that what she had done already was worth more than she could ever imagine, but she insisted. She went around her neck and pulled off an old, worn scapular[1]. Something Catholics receive at their first holy communion—two small pieces of cloth connected by a brown string. As she's taking it off, this

---

[1] Devotional scapulars are objects of popular piety, designed to show the wearers pledge to a Christian way of life. Also reminding the wearer of that promise.

woman tells me this was her father's who wore it every day towards the end of his life. That on his deathbed, he gave it to her, and now she was giving it to me. I again insisted that I couldn't take such a sentimental gift, but she forced it into my hands and said, "God wants you to have it." I held the holy sacramental in my hand in complete disbelief that all of this was happening, yet I couldn't deny this was indeed happening. She then gave me the warmest hug, took her dog, and bent the corner out of the grotto. I remember still kneeling a moment, but because of the significance of what had just happened, I got up and walked out of the grotto. She was gone.

The Meaning…

Looking back at it over the years, before being given answers about this experience shortly after getting into the paranormal, I tried to logically look at it. Okay, so she had to be a real woman headed to church at that hour whether I was going to be there or not, but how did she know I wanted to confess my sins? I didn't pray out loud, and I could've been there because of a dying relative or who knows what else. And why would this stranger give me this very special item from her dying father? Maybe she bent another corner quickly, but there really weren't many places to go once walking out of the grotto. Many details of that night baffled me and couldn't be explained other than it being a huge coincidence. But that night, I was shown something that still hasn't left me to this day, and even though many more spiritual experiences have happened to me since, this incident was the cornerstone in the foundation that is my faith today. That very special moment taught me that the Higher Power, the Source, which I choose to call God, heard my plea that night. That me wanting to speak to someone as bad as I did, my request to Him was so important that someone was sent. Also, that someone knew what it was I needed at that moment, and for good measure, I was to be given a physical memento. This was so I'd never forget or be able to discount the importance of that experience. To me, it felt like, whoever God was, was listening and He cared. I still have the scapular to this day and will pull it out from time to time.

The next day, I found myself driving the demolition car down to a rehab center. After a short stay and twelve-step meetings every day to follow, I found my first taste of hope. Quickly, I started to remember what being me felt like. I continued to attend meetings and began the process of working on myself. Seeing what made me tick, what I was afraid of, what I was still holding on to when it came to the past. I worked with a sponsor, someone who had some time in the program and had been through the Twelve Steps. Larry D. Groger, a spiritual giant. He's no longer physically here, but he definitely left his mark on the ones he worked with. He taught me that it was all about Love and Tolerance. I didn't understand that fully at the time, but the seed was planted, and I eternally thank Larry for that.

During this time, I was cleaning up the wreckage of the past seven years, working to pay back the money I stole, the property I damaged, and sort any legal trouble I had managed to get myself into. This included driving offenses and tickets. I was a pretty stubborn guy, especially when I was out there active in my addiction. I would get pulled over often, and if I got to leave the scene in my own car and not the cruiser, it was a good night. But no matter what, I'd always get a ticket. Those tickets I would always end up filing in the same folder every time. The "I don't give a shit" folder, and when tickets aren't paid, they eventually suspend your license. I remember I was only making two hundred and fifty dollars a week and could barely pay one thing at a time, but I was determined to do the right thing in all matters of my life. At the courthouse, paying a ticket one day, I was told to pay the big one, that the other tickets still had a few weeks left before they would affect my license. Later that week, I left a recovery meeting at night and got pulled over down the street. The red and blue flashing lights were a familiar sight and always brought on a quick case of the shakes, even when I was in the clear. The officer approached my vehicle and asked for my license, registration, and proof of insurance. I gave him all three confidently, and he went back to his cruiser.

A moment later, he returned and said, "Mr. Louis, can I get you to step out of the vehicle?" Never the words you want to hear when getting pulled over.

The Foxhole Prayer, my Second Spiritual Experience...

Now, to some, this incident may not seem like a big deal, and to others, it will sound crazy. But when that officer asked me to step out of the car, it was because my license came back as suspended. You mean the woman at the courthouse made a mistake when giving me that information about my license? Go figure, a county clerk making a mistake. Well, with the terrible driving record, past misdemeanor arrests, and unpaid fines, this severe offense of driving on a suspended license was going to get me a trip to the county jail. I couldn't believe it. Even when I was trying to do the right thing, I was still destined to be behind bars. They didn't want to hear anything about what the nice lady said at the courthouse. It was a "no pass go, straight to jail." A separate cop car came to get me as the tow truck pulled up to impound my vehicle. No pleading was getting me out of this one.

I was brought to the local police station to await the paddy wagon to take me to the county jail to be booked and processed. Who knows what trajectory this arrest was going to put me on, not to mention what it would do to my driving record. They put me in a holding cell and took my belt and shoelaces in case I wanted to hang myself. I sat there staring at the dirty, white walls hearing random echoes from officers passing by. Now, because of the way I had lived for as long as I did, I felt I still didn't deserve the mercy and grace of a loving Higher Power. But at this period in my life, I truly felt I was starting to recover and clean up my act. Why not a little grace in a tough spot? I got on my knees, and I remember saying, "Lord, God, I know you don't have to do this, but if there's any possible way to get me out of this one, I'd be very grateful." I made the sign of the cross, got up off my knees, and sat back on the cement bench next to the stainless steel toilet. Not more than a couple of minutes passed before an officer came in jangling those damn keys like Barney Fife and said, "I don't know, this must be your lucky day. We just got inundated with calls. The wagon can't come, and no one can take you to the county jail. We're just going to let you go. I'm going to take you back to where your car was and see if the tow truck driver can take you home."

In all the years interacting with law enforcement, I've never heard so many ridiculous things come out of an officer's mouth at one time. It was like out of a bad movie. He handed me my belt and laces, and quickly, I was in the backseat of the cruiser again, being whisked back to the scene of the arrest. Sure enough, my car had been loaded onto the flatbed, and I was let out to ask the driver if he'd drop me and my car off at my house. He looked as bewildered as I was and said, "Sure, hop in." Inside the cab of the truck, I told him of the ordeal, and he said he'd never seen anything like that. Then he told me he was new in recovery and was struggling a little bit with wanting to drink. I shared what little experience, strength, and hope I had up to that point, and right as he was dropping me off at my driveway, he told me what I said helped him a great deal and thanked me. I couldn't believe it. Not only was I spared execution at the last minute, so to speak, but I was also called on to help someone else with what I had learned so far.

What I took from that experience was that regardless of what other people's beliefs were, to me, it felt like Someone was listening to me when I prayed. Now, I'm not suggesting that when I asked for God to help, He then made multiple people commit crimes so that calls came into the station so I could be released. And anyone can make an argument that it was just a perfectly timed coincidence that worked in my favor. But after the church experience and now this holding-cell experience, I felt like whatever was out there was trying to get my attention in a very loving way.

I Move to Tampa...

After that, I continued to stay on the right path. I went to meetings, worked out, and got a job as a salesman at a wholesale jewelry company. Within a year, I had built up a savings any nineteen-year-old would be proud of. Being that all I ever really wanted to be was an entrepreneur, I eventually started a small jewelry business of my own with a friend. Working as a salesman with the previous wholesaler, I had made valuable contacts and learned quite a bit. With my rolodex of customers and a reliable supplier, nothing stood in our way. We bought our designs from a company in Tampa, so we decided to move there to be near the warehouse. I found a small apartment that wasn't in the best neighborhood, but hey, would you rent to me at that age after seeing my record? Neither would I. While living there, I would make the four-hour drive each month back to South Florida to visit friends and family. It was at a friend's house one weekend being back home that my first paranormal experience happened.

FIRST PARANORMAL EXPERIENCE

Every couple of months, I would get homesick and rent a car and drive across the state from Tampa back to Palm Beach County for the weekend. At this time, the business was doing well, and I had hired a secretary named Jen, who was a fellow Yankee fan like me and quickly became a good friend. On a few of these trips back home, Jen would accompany me. One particular night, an old high-school buddy, Brian, and his girlfriend, Catherine, invited us over for dinner. We gladly accepted. When we arrived, a very energetic Jack Russell Terrier named Spencer greeted us at the door. As we walked in, I noticed a Ouija board on the shelf tucked behind some books. Why I noticed this, I have no idea, but it stood out for some reason. I hadn't seen Brian in a few years, and it was good to see him. His girlfriend Cat was attending a Christian college at the time and was a sweet girl. After some catching-up, we all sat down and ate dinner. Afterward, we were sitting around the coffee table, and I chose to ask about the Ouija board. Immediately, Brian looked at Cat and then turned to me and said, "I don't want to talk about it." I told him he couldn't say something like that and expect me not to ask more questions. He told me that they had tried getting rid of it, throwing it away, but somehow it ended back in their house.

When I was seven back in Connecticut, the guy who used to cut our lawn told me you had to destroy a Ouija board to get rid of it. Why this landscaper told me this, I have no idea and for me to think he was an authority on Ouija boards made no sense. After hearing Brian tell us that, I still wasn't convinced our landscaper from fourteen years ago knew what he was talking about, so I asked Brian to pull it out as I had never used one before and was curious. He said no, but I kept asking, and it wasn't long before I was setting it up on the table. Brian wouldn't touch it, nor would Jen. But Cat, for some reason, agreed to try it with me. I remember saying a prayer beforehand as it just felt right to do so.

Nothing really happened for the first ten minutes as I asked who was with us and if anyone could use it. Brian and Jen sat there while Cat and I lightly laid our fingers on the edge of the planchette. Nothing happened. What a joke this thing was.

But then the plastic piece, part of this game manufactured by Hasbro and is ultimately sold as a novelty item for entertainment purposes, started to move ever so slightly. After Cat and I both asked each other for three minutes straight if either of us were moving it, the planchette started to move with purpose, finding letters instead of aimlessly moving from side to side. One of the first words it spelled was "H-E-L-L-O." A simple greeting. It continued for the next two hours and intensified until we couldn't handle it anymore. While I was approaching this section of the book, I wanted to make sure that what I had remembered about that night was accurate. So, I decided to call Brian. Mostly every experience I've had in this field is well documented through audio and video recordings. This, of course, happened when I wasn't involved in the field, so it wasn't documented. As you know, after some time, we can start to remember facts about an experience that didn't exactly happen. So, it's nice when there's someone else around to corroborate the story.

When I called him, we hadn't spoken in a couple of years. He is no longer with Cat and, of course, doesn't live in the same house anymore. Right away, I mentioned that I didn't expect him to remember much about that night, but he stopped me and told me he probably remembered more than I thought he did. I asked him why, and he told me that experience was burned into his memory. That he may not have remembered everything we asked the board that night, but he remembered enough. He remembers initially throwing the box out himself since the next day was trash day. Somehow it ended up back inside, and he thought that Cat must've brought it back in but claimed she would never have done that. They both wanted it gone. He remembers, as I do, it starting out slow but then it beginning to pick up with intensity. He remembers that with each spirit that used the planchette, it moved differently. One way it moved was in small circles to each letter. Other times, it would go from side to side to a letter and then on to the next. At times the planchette would leave our hands and move to the letters on its own and then stop. The first spirit pointed to numbers when asked about its age and then spelled a name when asked. It was claiming to be Cat's ex-boyfriend who died in a car accident. When she asked a question, the piece would move and spell a correct answer. Before the spirit left, it spelled "I- L-O-V-E- Y-O-U- C-A-T." She, of course, was crying hysterically as none of us expected anything like this.

Next, we asked for Brian's grandfather. With Brian staying on the couch and only Cat and I touching the planchette, he asked questions, and the board answered. From a simple question to what were his dying words, all the answers were correct. At the time, Brian didn't know what to say and seventeen years later still struggled to find a proper statement about it. At one point, he remembered the board continued to spell "B-A-L-L" over and over again. All four of us didn't know what exactly it meant as we intensely stared at the board. Finally, we heard whimpering behind the couch, and there was good ol' Spencer, Brian's dog staring up at the counter wanting his ball. We were too occupied to notice, and the spirit was letting us know.

But then something shifted. The questions weren't being answered anymore. Instead, statements were being made by the spirits, and they weren't that nice. I was called a derogatory name I won't repeat. Jen was told she was funny-looking, and with Cat getting the worst of it, she was told she likes a specific awkward sexual act done to her. When that happened, Cat threw the planchette across the room. By the way, when this happened, Brian was nervously laughing. I could tell the statement was true. Without realizing it, we had a full-on séance. At that point, I said, "We don't welcome any negativity," and the board said, "W-O-N-T - G-O... HAHAHA" and continued to go back and forth between the H and the A until we lifted our hands off the piece. I said Jesus Christ's name, and it ended there.

The Meaning...

After that, like Brian, that experience never left me either. What I learned that night was important. It answered questions, life-long questions for me. Because I'm the one that witnessed this paranormal activity firsthand, I knew there was definitely something more than this physical realm. That beyond the so-called "veil," there was something out there able to crudely communicate with us. These energies knew information that only our deceased loved ones and we only knew. I knew it wasn't an illusion, magic, or a trick our minds played on us. Others that weren't even participating witnessed it all and were equally blown away. Those were the FACTS. What did I believe? Well, I don't know what I believed. Was it really Cat's ex-boyfriend and Brian's grandad? I had no idea. What I knew was that the messages we were receiving at first were loving and positive. But then they were negative and hurtful. So, there were definitely two sides to this coin.

For weeks later, that experience was all I thought about. I talked to Jen about it back in Tampa, and it seemed to her it was a weird, unexplainable, and freaky experience. Therefore, she had nothing left to discuss. Time passed, and like most things in people's lives, out of sight, out of mind. I continued running my small company and focused on business. Slowly, I stopped doing the positive things that worked for me, which meant no more meetings. I started to get random anxiety attacks at different times of the day and had to see a doctor. They prescribed me a low dose prescription of Xanax, and I began taking the pills when I felt an attack come on. It wasn't long before I was abusing the medication. With the business starting to slow, it wasn't long before I started drinking again. I had been dry for about a year, and now I was falling back into that hole, but this time it felt like I was going deeper than ever before. When my prescriptions ran out because I abused them, I'd find the pills from a source on the street. An old guy named Butch I knew through a former employee would deliver them to my apartment. In the pill bottle one night, next to the Xanax, was a crack rock. I was addicted to cocaine in the past and knew what crack looked like, but I had never tried it before. What told me to try it that night, I don't know, but I did, and that started me on a path that would lead me to some of the darkest nights I've ever experienced.

I Was Back in Hell...

After another eight more months of being heavily addicted to multiple drugs, spending all the money I had left, catching a few new misdemeanors in Tampa, and destroying what was left of my business, I crawled back to South Florida on my hands and knees. My parents yet again were worried sick about their twenty-two-year-old derelict son and didn't have the means to send me to another rehab. Living in a small apartment with help from my residual income and my father, I tried attending meetings again. But I'd just go home after the meeting, fall to temptation, and drink whatever I could get my hands on. Ready to die but too much of a coward to do it myself, I was hoping every night that the drugs would do the job and just kill me off.

One night, an old high-school friend picked me up with his girlfriend's old Dodge Neon that he took without her knowing. He wasn't exactly on a winning streak himself, and you know the saying, misery loves company. I still owned a small 22. cal handgun from when I turned twenty-one, and I decided to bring that along with me just in case it got dangerous. I figured we'd be out all night buying drugs—who knows what could happen.

MY LIFE WAS ABOUT TO CHANGE

After a night of smoking and drinking whatever we could get our hands on, the sun was starting to come up, and we knew this fantastic night of misery was coming to an end. With only twenty bucks left in our pocket, we decided to pull down a street known for selling dope and saw a dealer standing on the corner. I signaled to him we were looking to buy as he approached the driver's side window. He dropped forty dollars' worth of rock in my hand, and I gave him the folded twenty. My friend, who was driving the vehicle, went to pull off, and before we could realize what was happening, the dealer jumped headfirst inside the car, and we were in an all-out blow-for-blow struggle. Fighting a man who was 6'2" and around 240lbs, I was falling on the losing side of the battle and had to do something quickly.

I went for the glove compartment and grabbed my pistol. I then put my foot on his chest and pushed him up against the inside of the windshield, where I unloaded my gun, working my way up his body shooting him six times. The seventh shot that was aimed for his head jammed as he managed to break the windshield and land on the hood of the car. Blood and glass were everywhere, and our ears were ringing from shooting the gun inside the vehicle, but this was not the time to act stunned. My friend got out, grabbed the man by his pants, and dragged his lifeless body off the car. At the same time, the dealer's friends jumped into a truck and started to come after us. My buddy jumped back in the car, and with no windshield and two busted tires, we raced to the police station to turn ourselves in. We knew things didn't end well in high-speed pursuits, so we ended it there. We were taken into custody and charged with attempted murder. Luckily, the dealer survived.

If That Wasn't Enough…

Sitting in jail for a few days, the state of Florida decided not to file charges against me due to the fact that the gun was legal, even though I admitted to buying drugs. It was ruled self-defense. Did I deserve that kind of leniency? Probably not, but the fact that the guy I shot was a convicted child molester with an extensive criminal history probably helped when the time came to make that decision. Regardless, it wouldn't matter because what I did thirty days after the shooting would guarantee me a trip to a Florida State penitentiary.

In 2004, a string of four hurricanes hit Florida within six weeks' time that would leave the state reeling from the destruction with over $45 billion in damage. First was Charley, a Category 4 storm, then Frances, a Cat 2 with Ivan and Jeanne, both barreling through as Cat 3s. A few days after being released from jail, hurricane Frances hit Palm Beach County, and I was able to ride out the storm with Jen and her family in Tampa. After all I had put her through, I don't know why she let me stay with her, but I was grateful. Of course, I was still numb to the shooting, and there was no desire at that point to fix my life in any way. I truly just wanted to die and felt I was like a cockroach, impervious to any immediate destruction.

I went back to Palm Beach County with not much to live for. There I sat in a dark apartment alone, finding ways to obtain some kind of cheap alcohol and drink myself into a stupor each night. Thirty days after being pummeled by hurricane Frances, hurricane Jeanne was expected to crash right through us. This time I wasn't going to run to the west coast of Florida to escape it, and my family again wanted nothing to do with me. So I said screw it, I'll ride the storm out in my shitty apartment, and I'll be fine. I'll get some supplies and be okay, but I wasn't thinking about batteries and bottled water. Nope, I needed booze, pills, and anything else that would anesthetize the pain and help me forget the present threat of Jeanne.

The storm approached, and like any other hurricane, the wind slowly starts to increase in speed. Once it reaches a steady 140mph, the wind howls like a ravenous animal looking for meat to consume. It bends and snaps trees, picks up roofs, turns debris into deadly missiles, and drops crazy amounts of rain, not to mention the storm surges. With conditions worsening by the minute, it wouldn't be long before the power would go out, and what I just described would be a reality. All of a sudden, my phone rang, and it was another old acquaintance, one I hadn't seen in ages and, honestly, it could've stayed that way. Here was another guy, who up to this point had done nothing with his life and was seeking refuge from the storm last minute, most likely because no one wanted him at their house. I sure knew how to pick friends, let me tell you. I told this fellow degenerate he could come over but that my "supplies" were just for me, that there was none for him. He agreed and somehow made it over to my apartment, and while we sat there with the storm raging at its full strength, I broke down and allowed him some of the last of my stash.

Before I knew it, we were completely out, and the only reasonable thing to do was try and get a hold of a drug dealer. A different one, of course, from the one I shot. Now, forget the fact that there was a life-threatening, catastrophic natural disaster happening outside. The comedown from amphetamines is way worse, in my opinion. I remember, when copping my last score from the couple that lived a few buildings over, hearing them say they were going to evacuate for the storm. Being that my friend consumed the last of my goodies, the only reasonable thing to do at this point was to break into the couple's house and steal their stash.

As we made our way outside through three feet of water and 100mph wind, we resembled something close to Laurel and Hardy. I was so thin from the constant drug use I was being blown back by the wind and could barely walk. It took my friend, who was certainly not lacking meat on his bones, to hold on to me until we reached the dealer's second-floor apartment. Once we reached the top of the stairs, I knocked and called out to see if they were home. I heard nothing. Again, I knocked hard, with no one coming to the door. I raised my foot and readied myself to kick it in when suddenly, it opened. Standing there stunned with my foot in the air like the Karate Kid, I see three people holding pipes and broken broomsticks in their hands. Immediately I take a swift broomstick to the head with what I can only assume was one of the pipes to follow. As I'm bleeding from the head and start to lose consciousness, I feel a hand grab me by the shirt and begin to drag me inside the apartment. Knowing I probably would die a painful death in there, I grabbed the banister, and while being beaten and stripped naked, I dragged myself down the stairs and somehow hobbled back home without taking any more hits.

My accomplice, being a very large fellow, as I mentioned, somehow was able to run faster than any 300lbs man I'd ever seen. He was already back in my apartment by the time I stumbled in, bleeding, and almost naked. I could barely muster up enough strength to tell him to call 911 before falling and passing out. Thankfully, the pillow I was lying on helped stop the bleeding as it took two hours before the ambulance would finally reach me due to the storm. When I was brought into the hospital, I was asked what happened. Without giving it too much thought, I told the paramedics a tree fell on me. It seemed like the answer sufficed until I saw my large friend being wheeled in on a gurney with a smashed face and neck brace on. Next to him, talking in his ear, stood a plain-clothed detective, all the while never taking his eyes off me. All I could think was, I just left this guy in my apartment perfectly fine, now he's clinging to life. What the hell happened?

It wasn't long before the detective made his way over to inform me that after the ambulance brought me to the hospital, my buddy couldn't find his car keys and went back around to the apartment we just tried to rob to look for them. Somehow the dealers saw him, chased him down, and beat him pretty badly as well. Once in the hospital, he told the detective everything, and it was me who, rightfully so, was going back to jail.

Upon arriving at the county jail, I was told that not only was I being charged with burglary of an occupied dwelling during a state of emergency, a charge that carries a 20-year sentence, but that I'd also be charged with attempted murder from the shooting 30 days prior. My face turned white, and I was immediately put on suicide watch and held without bond. In one of my first appearances in court, the public defender came up to me and said, "Because of the shooting, you'll be facing life in prison. I can cut you a deal today for 20 years, and I suggest you take it." I didn't take that deal that day and opted to sit in jail and take my chances at trial. The first thing I needed to do was find a better attorney.

ABSOLUTE ROCK BOTTOM

At this point, my father was barely talking to me. The thought of his only son spending life in prison was apparently too much for him to bear, so he again spent the little bit of money he had on hiring me a decent attorney. But with two violent crimes, one during a state of emergency, there wasn't much he could do. Still, with no bond, all I could do was sit in the county jail and watch the Boston Red Sox come back from a three-game deficit in the playoffs, something that's never been done before, to beat the Yankees and go on to win the World Series. A dark, dark time.

From there, I sat for an additional seven months, and at the eleventh hour, the state requested more time to prepare their case. So, I was allowed to await my trial at home on house arrest. I knew I didn't have much of a chance at trial but was prolonging the inevitable for as long as I could. To me, there was really no hope; I was going to go to prison and for a really long time. My thought was, even if I got a deal, I would be offered ten years, and a decade behind bars is a pretty long time.

With this kind of thinking, I said, screw it and started to find ways to drink and get high in my apartment without leaving. Other degenerates like myself would bring supplies over for an inflated cost, and I didn't care. I ended up selling every possession I had until the TV was the last to go, and once it went, I stared at the wall where it used to be. The charges were eventually dropped against my buddy who was with me on the shooting as I was the real trigger man and my portly friend who morphed into a track star during the robbery agreed to testify against me in exchange for leniency on his sentence. I knew this time I wasn't just going to find a way out of this mess. I was going to have to face whatever came my way.

Sitting in my empty, dirty apartment, barely eating, just awaiting my fate, I understood what complete hopelessness felt like. There was no point in even trying. I gave up, and this was the absolute lowest I had ever been. But with that surrender came a liberating feeling, and something changed. Just like that night at the church grotto crying out to God for help, the energy shifted, and I received help. After being offered nothing less than twenty years from the state, the case changed prosecutors. My attorney knew the new prosecutor assigned to the case, and just like that, I was being sentenced to two and a half years in prison instead. Now, I'm not saying once I became fully broken, God fired a lawyer and hired a different one so I could get off, but nothing had been working out up to that point. Within a week of internally surrendering, I received the call from my attorney, and I took the deal.

On June 17th, 2005, I was shipped off to a maximum-security Florida state prison and was officially the property of the Dept. of Corrections. Surrounded by some of Florida's nastiest killers and rapists, I spent my time reading, working out, and drawing. I would charge a modest fee (two instant soups and a candy bar) to draw portraits for inmates to send home to their families. I was also able to get a job in the sewing room, making stuffed teddy bears for Toys for Tots. I never knew how to sew, but because the sewing room was the only place on the compound that had air conditioning, I convinced the female guard that I was a quick learner and got hired. I got so good I could sew and stuff up to 22 bears a day. When I wasn't working, or on the prison yard, I would attend Twelve Step meetings when they were offered. Sometimes no one would bring a meeting in, and I'd find another inmate or two to sit with, Big Book in hand, and have a meeting ourselves. I knew I never wanted to be the way I was, and if I followed these simple steps, one day at a time, I would never have to be.

An Evil Presence, My Second Paranormal Experience...
Early into my sentence, something pivotal happened to me while locked in my cell overnight. In the middle of the Florida everglades in the dead of summer (just reminding you, no air conditioning), I was lying on my bunk trying to sleep in a six-by-nine cell that must have been 100 degrees. It was around three in the morning, and I was drifting in and out of sleep due to the heat. I then all of a sudden felt something very dark, very malevolent inside the cell with me. An immense pressure built up in my head, and it started throbbing, like a migraine, but faster than

any headache I had ever felt come on me. I remember thinking, without a doubt, something was there with me, and it didn't feel human. It was attacking me somehow, smothering me in a way where the only thing I could do was call out to Jesus Christ and rebuke whatever it was in His name. All I remember was feeling a sense of peace wash over me, and the pain in my head subsided as I slipped into a peaceful sleep.

Whatever it was, and I'm not convinced it wasn't a demon, it just left and couldn't do anything to me after I called out to Jesus for help. Now, remember, even though I had been blessed that lowly night at the church grotto, spared in the holding cell, and given mercy with a greatly reduced prison sentence, the idea of a personal connection to God was still foreign to me due to what I had gone through in my life. I had lost touch with what I thought God was to me, and ever since the Ouija experience at Brian's, I hadn't had any other paranormal encounters since. But intrinsically, I knew to call out to Jesus. Feeling this dark entity, whatever it was, and finding relief from calling out Jesus's name, was a moment that certainly shaped my faith. I began to start praying more and incorporating Jesus in my prayers each time. Because prison was so very painful, I couldn't spend one day locked up in vain. That meant I had to make every day count, and when the day came that I was to be released, I could never fall back into the booze and drugs again, or I'd end up back behind the wall. With the recidivism rate at roughly 90%, that meant that if I was to make it, I would have to fall into that 10 percentile. The relapse rate was the same in recovery, and the odds were stacked against me, this I knew.

Another Miracle...

With only a little over 60 days left of my sentence, I was sent closer to home to a work-release camp. This meant technically I'd still be in prison, but Monday through Friday, I'd be allowed to ride a bike to a job and work. Once my shift was over, I'd have to ride back to the prison. Most inmates transferred to a work release camp find a job at one of the set packing houses, warehouses, or landscape companies the prison has already lined up in advance. When I arrived, there wasn't a set job available for me, so they allowed me to try and find one on my own. I had to call businesses from the prison payphone, and line up interviews. I'd then have to let the prison know where the interviews were, and when I showed up, I'd have to call the prison to check-in. It wasn't easy, not to mention that most businesses didn't want to hire a violent convicted felon. I knew if I could land a job at a restaurant, I could have my first decent meal in two years.

I called the closest place I could find, which was an Applebee's, and lined up an interview. When I showed up to the interview, I looked like I had just jumped into a pool with my clothes on; it was that hot out. I had to explain my situation, and for whatever reason, they liked me, and I was hired. I'd work my butt off every night and make sure to order myself a steak at the end of my shift. While I was eating sizzling fajitas and Bourbon Street steaks, the guys back at the prison were eating meat surprise sandwiches that we all knew weren't meat. After the shift, I would ride back to the prison, and if I was lucky, another server with a big trunk would throw my bike in the back and drop me off a block away so I wouldn't get in trouble. Sometimes, I'd be able to sneak chicken tenders and hamburgers over the fence for some of my fellow inmates. I was even able to get my cellmate, Bobby, a job cooking on the line.

One night after our shift, Bobby and I were riding our bikes back to the prison center. It was my last week there, and we were taking a different route each night to prolong going back. Pedaling down a back street with no traffic, in a flash, my bike was lifted off the ground as I found myself on the windshield of a van going 45mph. The momentum of the hit sent me rolling off the windshield into the air and coming back down onto the roof of the van. I then rolled off the roof and landed in the street headfirst. The van sped off, never even tapping the brakes in an attempt to slow down or stop. Staring up at the sky, not knowing if I was dead or paralyzed, all I heard was, "Holy shit Josh, are you okay?" I began to wiggle my fingers and toes and then started patting myself all over to check. Bobby helped me up, and the first words out of my mouth were, "Thank you, God." Somehow I just survived a direct hit from behind by a van doing almost 50mph. The bike was completely destroyed.

When we got back to the prison, Bobby shared the story with the other inmates, and for the remainder of my time at the Fort Pierce Work Release Center, I was known as Boy Wonder. To this day, I still don't understand the physics behind the collision and how I walked away completely unscathed, but I credit it to a Higher Power. Call it Divine intervention or just a lucky hit, but to me, it was a miracle.

Starting Again from the Bottom…

Upon my release, I ended up receiving time served for the eight months I did in the county and time off for good behavior. I served a total of twenty-two months, and in October of 2006, I was released. I had no job, no car, no place to live, and my father, as loving as he was, told me I had only three days of staying with him before I needed to find a room to rent somewhere else. He would help me with the first month, but after that, I was on my own. I quickly found a job at a deli and still attended Twelve Step meetings after my shifts, often falling asleep in the back of the room from working doubles. I took the bus wherever I needed to go and found a small efficiency to rent. It wasn't much, but I was happy—I was free. Everything meant so much more to me, especially the little things. Not to mention, I hadn't had a drink or anything else for that matter in over two years, and that's the way it was going to stay.

Now, I won't go into too much detail regarding everything I did after prison. But I must share the pivotal moments, the turning points in my life that led me to where I am today. Because of the intense and destructive way I previously lived, I felt I had already lived two lives within this one existence. But to me, this meant I was changing for the better. As I continued to attend Twelve Step meetings, I worked with other guys just released from prison and shared with them what I had learned. I took speaking commitments, where I would share with juveniles who were not yet stuck in the system about how miserable prison was and why it was smart to stay out. This kind of service empowered me, and I saw how it helped others.

Eventually, I quit my deli job and started a small financial company with an old friend. Together, we secured a small office above the deli I used to work at and, within six months, I was able to hire a few people. It was very successful, and shortly after, I got my driver's license back, a new car, and a better apartment, all the while still attending meetings. I knew if meetings ever took a backseat as they did in Tampa, I could save myself some time and just drive that new car to the prison and turn myself in again. I wasn't going to make the same mistake I made last time. In addition to having the financial company, I saw a small space in the downtown area and decided to open up a hookah bar. Hookah is a Middle Eastern tobacco pipe like the one the caterpillar smokes in *Alice in Wonderland*. I had been to one once before, and with no drinking involved, I really enjoyed it. It was an immediate hit, and people would come and sit, smoke, and relax while they listened to music.

I FINALLY ARRIVED

Eventually, I realized there wasn't a lot of profit in people smoking a fifteen-dollar hookah for two hours, and I started looking at other options to infuse money into the business. After some online digging, I found a novelty item being sold overseas in Europe known as herbal incense. Basically a form of synthetic marijuana that people enjoyed as an alternative to the real thing. Just because I didn't drink or do anything that was mind-altering, didn't mean others had to abstain as well. I imported the product and began selling it in my bar. It went gangbusters, and it wasn't long before I became one of the biggest distributors of the stuff in the US. I was selling the product to head shops, hookah bars, and convenience stores in most states.

Still owning the financial company, the hookah bar, and now a major distribution company, I was pulling in over a million dollars a year. This was the kind of money people dreamed of making, and I was enjoying every minute of it—new cars, properties, clothes, lavish dinners, trips, and memberships at haughty golf clubs. It was a pretty good life for a convicted felon, who had barely earned his GED. When it came to the distribution company, I made sure to hire every friend and family member I could and grossly overpaid them. It was a great feeling; I felt I had arrived.

Of course, throughout it all, I still continued to go to meetings and help people within the program any chance I could. I continued to attend therapy and work on deeply rooted issues within myself. I worked the Twelve Steps with a sponsor and properly made amends to friends and family for the past transgressions I committed. This meant paying off any debt I had accrued over the last ten years. I even met a beautiful girl one night at my hookah bar named Nicolette, and just like that, we began dating. In my opinion, I was living a life second to none, and to top it off, the Yankees won their 27th Championship that year.

FIRST CONSCIOUS INTUITIVE FEELING...

All was going perfectly. I couldn't imagine it any better. One Sunday night driving home from the hookah bar, I stopped at a 7-Eleven to get some gas and noticed a car sitting by a pump not pumping any gas. It was strange, but I didn't pay any more attention to it. At the time, I was living in a huge house with my business partner and knew he'd be asleep when I got home. When I pulled into the driveway, I got out and began walking up to the door. Now, I don't know if it was my sixth sense already kicking in or what, but I felt someone about to come up behind me right then. Instinctively, I turned around in a defensive fighting position, and sure enough, a man with a gun and a mask was coming at me from the shadows.

Maybe it was all the years of Karate as a kid and getting my ass kicked in the schoolyard, coupled with the two years in prison, but I turned into Jackie Chan and did all kinds of moves on my assailant. I was about to gain control of the gun when three more just like him ran out from each side of the bushes and grabbed me. Immediately I was brought inside as two of them gained access to my business partner's room. As I heard the struggle ensue in the other room, I again turned on my captors and fought. This time I was pistol-whipped in the head and suffered a broken hand. They took cash, some jewelry, and the shotgun my business partner tried to wield before they over-powered him. Once they had what they came for, they were out the front door, into a getaway car, and gone.

At the hospital, I received staples in my head and a cast on the arm. The detectives asked me if I thought it might have been anyone I knew, stating that 85% of the time, a robbery like this was an inside job. I couldn't think of anyone in particular. Still, together with the private investigators I hired to work with the police, we found out that a disgruntled former employee had set me up. Months later, three of the four men that committed the robbery were caught using my business partner's shotgun in another crime.

Pigs Get Fed, Hogs Get Slaughtered ...

At this time, others had come into the industry and started committing dangerous acts. That was never the point for me when I got involved, but that's what it had become. It was time for me to hang it up, and so I plotted my exit. I told friends and family I was done, I sold the company to a guy in Texas, and with enough money to take some time off for a while, that's exactly what I did. My partner and I also decided to sell the financial company, but still held on to the hookah bar. Of course, it reverted to the chill place it once was before the incense wave hit, and Nikki and I were now living in a new house I'd purchased as we were expecting our first child. Where else was this wild ride called life going to take me now?

Lights, Camera, Action...

Ever since getting out of prison, I had been secretly working on a script for a film involving my story. I felt this was a perfect time in my life to follow a true passion of mine. I even created a room in my new house dedicated just to finishing the script. I set up chairs and put up movie posters of films I grew up loving: *Butch Cassidy and the Sundance Kid*, *The Big Lebowski*, *Goodfellas*, *Terminator 2*, the *Matrix* trilogy, and, of course, *Superman*. The Christopher Reeves version and not the CGI garbage that canceled out real movie-making. My best friend, Chris, would come over every day, and together, we completed the screenplay. With a budget of a little over $300k, I was going to finance most of the film myself along with a few other investors. We titled the film *Not For Human Consumption*[2], and with a rough draft, we flew out to Hollywood and began taking meetings with casting directors and potential crew members. This was going to be a full-length feature film, and even though the budget was ultra-low for Hollywood's standards, it was certainly enough for a kid with a lifelong dream of making movies.

Eventually, with a finished script, financing in place, a cast and crew hired, we shot the film. Down here in Palm Beach County, it took almost a month of shooting every day, sometimes twenty-hour days to complete. It was one of the most exciting times of my life. Nikki and I had the baby, and we welcomed little miss Eva Monroe into the world just as the film was going into post-production. Once the film was locked and we had a final cut, we began submitting it to film festivals in different parts of the country. We felt it wouldn't be long before we could start talking to viable distributors to fully release the film.

The Stage Is Set...

Enjoying the fruits of my labor, I had a few small properties I was renting out, the hookah bar was still thriving, and Nikki and I were excited about being new parents. Early on, we took Eva to Disney World, zoos, and even purchased a small boat to cruise the intra-coastal waterway on the weekends. I seriously felt retired at age 31, and why not? I felt like I had accomplished so much in the time since being released from prison. Life was good, and if you had asked me six years earlier while sitting in a cell, what I thought my life would look like after I got out, I certainly wouldn't

---

[2] To watch *Not For Human Consumption* the movie, it is available on most major platforms. Visit www.magicflamefilms.com for more viewing options.

have thought it would've looked like this. There's a line in the Big Book of Alcoholics Anonymous on page 25. It states,

> *"We have found much of heaven, and we have been rocketed into the fourth dimension of existence of which we had not even dreamed."*

Well, that's how I felt and what I didn't realize was everything I had been through up to that point set the stage for something much bigger to happen.

THE NEXT CHAPTER

The next chapter in my spiritual journey

SO THERE I WAS. IT was 2012, my movie *"Not For Human Consumption"* was being submitted to film festivals all over the country, and I was working on a new script. Financially, I was good for a while, and I was spending more time working on helping people within Twelve Step programs. When I wasn't managing my hookah bar or at a meeting, I was with my family. It was an amazing time.

One night, Nikki and I were flipping through channels looking for something to watch on TV and landed on a paranormal show. We saw one of the characters, who was clearly overdramatizing everything, holding a device that looked like a small hand-held radio. He was trying to use this device to communicate with the dead. This is known as ITC[3] (Instrumental-Trans Communication), which is the use of a device or instrument to communicate with paranormal entities. Once in a while, a short, static-filled sound would come through the small box, and on the screen, a caption would appear displaying what they thought it said. The idea behind this was that the spirit could take the short bits of sound coming from the fast scanning radio and manipulate the audio to form their own responses. Sometimes it would be a clear, unmistakable reply and the caption seemed correct, sometimes it was hard to hear. We didn't know what to believe, but I quickly thought of my Ouija board experience over at Brian's many years before. Regardless of what I saw when

---

[3] In the next chapter I cover ITC more thoroughly. See sub-chapter *History of Instrumental Trans-Communication*, pages 97 & 98.

watching these shows, I knew that the Ouija board experience really happened. That was a true paranormal experience for me.

A couple of weeks later, Nikki had a video pulled up on YouTube of someone trying to use the same hand-held radio that was used on the show we saw. Again, we heard very quick, difficult-to-understand responses coming through this little device. Out of five replies, we'd maybe hear one that was discernible enough to actually understand it. This piqued both of our interests though and while sitting in our chairs out back or in our garage, we'd watch videos of people dabbling in spirit communication on YouTube. While searching for other channels, Nikki found Steve Huff of Huff Paranormal[4], a pioneer in spirit communication. It was weird, I remember hearing his voice from one of his videos and not yet seeing him, I thought, *Wow, that guy kind of sounds like me.* Steve hadn't had his channel up for long at that point and was experimenting with that same hand-held radio spirit box as well as other small radios that had been hacked to perform like the one on that show. He was getting "above-average" results.

Another method we saw on TV and these YouTube channels, were people using regular voice recorders to capture EVP[5] (Electronic Voice Phenomenon), a voice response captured from thin air. These responses were hard to hear, but every once in a while, someone would capture what would be considered a Class-A EVP, an unmistakably clear response. The recorders used were not expensive, being regular brand names from any store. The radios were easily hacked to get them to operate as a scanning spirit box.

---

[4] To learn more about Steve Huff, see chapter *Influential People - Steve Huff*, page 180.
[5] Electronic Voice Phenomena (EVP) are sounds found on electronic recordings that are interpreted as spirit voices that have been either unintentionally recorded or intentionally requested and recorded.

So, not really knowing what the deal was, I purchased what any new ghost hunter starts out with: a PSB7 spirit box (a cheaply made radio to scan quickly through radio stations), a digital RCA voice recorder, and a K2 meter. The meter was a simple hand-held EMF[6] meter with lights on it that indicated electromagnetic waves in the environment around us. If you hold one of these meters near a cell phone or power outlet, the meter will spike. So trying to use these around electric devices makes it difficult, but spirits can interact with them. With these items that cost a total of $150, we began to experiment.

Nikki and I were a bit apprehensive because the only real paranormal knowledge we had been given was from the drama-filled reality shows and movies. But again, I mention Steve Huff. He was someone speaking to the spirits in a polite manner, always respectful and this completely resonated with me. It made sense that if these were souls that used to be in a body, we were the same. So why provoke or act like spirits were Bigfoot? But what about the idea that all spirits on the other side are just demons emulating loved ones that are trying to possess our bodies?[7] We really felt we needed to proceed carefully.

We made sure to go to well-lit parks and public areas to test the gear, and when we did, we didn't stay long. It was as if I was approaching the veil, the one that separates this world and the other side. I wasn't sure how far I wanted to go or how much I really wanted to know. But one night, after visiting a park known for being a mass grave of hurricane victims from 1928, I listened to my audio recordings when I got home. Lo and behold,

---

[6] Electromagnetic waves or EM waves are waves that are created as a result of vibrations between an electric field and a magnetic field. These waves are composed of oscillating magnetic and electric fields.

[7] This misunderstanding stems from misinterpreting certain bible verses. To understand more, see chapter *Proof in the Bible*, page 151, 2nd paragraph.

a clear response through the spirit box saying, "Help me!" I played it for Nikki, and she heard it as well. *Wow, what a feeling.* At that moment, it did two things for me, it confirmed there was something on the other side able to communicate with us, and the idea of some spirits getting "stuck" in the afterlife seemed like a reality now.

From there, I was pretty much hooked. I knew what I had discovered was real—not a show, or a horror movie, or some dramatized story passed down from one family member to another. These recordings were real scientific findings in researching life after death, and now I knew the truth, or at least a very small fraction of it. When Nikki and I could get a babysitter, we'd go out on the weekends and continue to conduct our novice investigations. When someone like Steve Huff would try a new radio or technique, I'd try it as well and find that, most of the time, I would get the same "above-average" results.

It was Nikki's birthday, and I decided to take her down to Key West for the weekend. We packed a couple of light bags and jumped in the car to drive that five-and-a-half-hour drive down the two-lane road known as US-1. Of course, I brought my ghost-hunting kit with me and even downloaded an app on the phone. Now, before you say, "An app? On the phone?" Yes. Even though it sounds crazy and too easy to get false positives (results showing something is present when it's not), it's smart to investigate all tools and techniques to see what works. This particular app was something called an Ovilus. An Ovilus is a program or device that stores words in a bank. The idea is the spirit can access that word bank and, in a sense, pluck the word it wants to use to communicate. It sort of sounds like that old Speak & Spell toy we used as kids—kind of creepy and robotic sometimes.

Sunday night, April 14th, 2013, I sat on the hotel's balcony watching the sunset as a cruise ship was getting ready to come into port. I decided to set my phone up on the balcony and record the sunset as that was something I've always wanted to do. I really loved messing with videos and making little montages; it was fun and expressive. While I was sitting there in the dark, editing the video, something told me to turn on the Ovilus.

Earlier in the day, Nikki and I had brought the gear to the old Key West cemetery and captured very little. But I thought maybe something would come through here at the hotel. I opened the Ovilus and just sat there, looking out at the ocean melt into the endless backdrop of the black night sky. I asked the first phrase that comes to every ghost hunter or paranormal investigator who begins doing this type of thing, which is, "Is anybody there?" I got nothing. Then I started to see the letters look like they were getting ready to form a word. I said, "Oh, here we go, what nonsense is this thing going to say?" I felt maybe it was like the Magic 8-Ball. It then spit out the words "CROWD," "EXPLOSION," "TOMORROW," and "BLOOD." I thought it to be strange but turned it off and went to bed.

Monday, April 15th, 2013, the next morning. We woke up late and prepared to check out of the hotel. We finally left and got on the road a little after 2 PM. Heading back home, traveling over the 7 Mile Bridge, we hear on the news, there was a bombing at the Boston Marathon killing three people and injuring hundreds of others. I showed Nikki the responses from the Ovilus. We were speechless.

I tell you that story because whether it was a fluke or actual energy interacting with the app to give responses relevant to future events, there was always something that would happen that kept me seeking. This, of course, was one of those moments. I decided that week I was going to start a YouTube channel and start displaying the evidence I was capturing. My first video would be the sunset I recorded in Key West on the balcony. It had nothing to do with the paranormal but what happened afterward with the Ovilus was definitely a turning point for me.

Earlier in the week, before going to the Keys, I was at the point where I wanted to do more with the voices I heard on the recordings. Nikki and I had already been to enough locations where we could record plenty of responses asking for help. What could we do to help, though? Being a person who had learned to ask his Higher Power for help, I prayed to God that if there was something I could do, to please show me. It was as simple as that. I figured I would exercise what the Twelve Steps had taught me and turn it over to a power greater than myself. I then would move my feet in the direction I was inspired to follow and trust the results. Remember, this wasn't something I was accustomed to doing. Because of the spiritual experiences in the past, where blind faith in an unseen power had worked, I was practicing it more and more.

INTRODUCED TO A MEDIUM

A few days after asking for that help, I was speaking to a friend about what we were finding in these cemeteries and mausoleums. He then mentioned he knew someone who was a medium, someone who speaks with the dead. I couldn't believe it. Of course, I had seen the likes of John Edwards, Sylvia Brown, and others on TV in the past, but I had no firsthand experience with any kind of psychic or medium. He gave me her number and told me to give her a call. Her name was Connie Fox[8], and she had been a practicing intuitive for the past 20 years.

The next day, I gave her a call, and we met for coffee. She was so kind and had such a wonderful energy about her. She told me that she didn't see or feel things; that she is clairaudient. This means she just intuitively hears the spirit speak to her internally. I nodded, and told her this was all new to me. I asked her if she would come out with us one night to a cemetery or even in the lot behind my hookah bar, as the building was very old and used as a brothel at one point. She agreed, and we planned a night to meet.

I had already picked up the name Mike along with a few others behind the bar in previous sessions. These were names that came up on the recorders, spirit boxes, and even the Ovilus, some

---

[8] To learn more about Connie Fox, see chapter *Influential People - Connie Fox*, page 179.

of them asking for help. Fun fact: one of those recordings from the PSB7 spirit box said, "All hope gone," or at least that's what I heard. It was that response that inspired me to name our little group H.O.P.E., an acronym for Helpers of Paranormal Entities. This felt fitting because all I wanted to do was help them. By inviting Connie to meet us, I was hoping she'd pick up on some of the names at that location without any information from me whatsoever. It was a long shot but worth a try.

Out behind my hookah bar, I had my spirit box, EMF meter, as well as a voice recorder ready to go. I told her nothing and asked if she could connect with the spirits there that have asked for help in the past. Immediately, she picked up on the name Mike. It was that quick. If I didn't witness it firsthand, I probably wouldn't believe it. Nikki and I were amazed. I asked if this Mike had anything he wanted to say. Then with a certain delivery, not too dramatic but somewhat emphatic, she channels the words "Thank you for coming back." At this point, a lot is going through my head, like, how is this possible? I continued to go with it as I asked Mike if he was one of the spirits asking for help. Speaking for Mike, Connie replies, "Yes, yes, what do I need to do? There's no light." I looked at Connie and asked her if there was anything she knew we could do.

She had never gone out on a ghost hunt before. Her readings with clients mostly consisted of intuitive health readings, an occasional passed loved one, or a channeled angel for divine messages. Dealing with stuck spirits was something she hadn't encountered much in the past, and when she did, she would just say a prayer.

While sitting in old folding chairs behind my bar in the dark, Connie proceeded to tell us she had an angel she called J. that she channeled regularly. It was right then when she asked this angel my question—if we could help these spirits. With a softer, gentler delivery came forth a response to talk to Mike for a moment and let him share his pain. Have him ask out loud for God when he's ready. Connie then went back to connecting with Mike while I had the spirit box running, hoping to pick up something to validate any of what was going on. At that point, I began to have a conversation with Mike the same I would have a conversation with anyone who was alive. It felt like there was no communication barrier, and Mike explained that he never saw the Light when he died. Or even really knew much about God, but he had heard of Jesus, he said.

All of the answers I gave him came naturally due to all the years of working the Twelve Steps, helping guys less fortunate than me through their pain, and the spiritual experiences I had along the way. Even though he was happier talking to us, he had little to no faith and was scared. With a little compassion and understanding from us, it wasn't long before Mike was willing to ask for a God of his understanding, at one point, even saying the name Jesus Christ. Connie, who was just kind of staring blankly as she channeled Mike's words, paused. A brief moment of quiet passed, and then came the words, "A man! I see a man. He's beautiful. Light, I see bright light." At that moment, we heard the word "light" come through the spirit box. It wasn't long before Nikki, and I heard Connie channel "Thank you, thank you" just as a "Thank you" was heard coming through the box as well.

I then turned off the equipment, and we all just sat there a moment, wondering what we had just witnessed in this dimly lit parking lot. I asked Connie if Mike was gone. Checking back in with her angel J., in a soft tone, different from Connie's own cadence, she delivered the answer, "Yes, Connie, Mike has left. Thank you, to each of you."

I have to tell you, whether or not that truly happened in the spirit realm and a spirit named Mike really crossed over, or whether it was all Connie's imagination producing Mike and J.'s words, we couldn't deny what came through the box, and we all felt amazing. We all felt something very special just happened. The fact that Connie picked up on Mike's name before being given any information, and the validating responses that came through the box were enough to ask her to come back out with us for another session.

The next time we would meet up again as a group was to investigate the Devil's Tree in Port St. Lucie, which became the first real paranormal video posted on the channel. This ominous tree was located at a county park deep in the woods and was known to be a hot spot for paranormal activity. Many verifiable horrible acts happened at this tree. The session there was very emotional and would later become the inspiration for my second feature film.[9]

I'll also point out something I was only able to see in hindsight. After finding ghost hunting as a hobby and quickly discovering it was more than that, I asked my Higher Power to bring us some kind of direction. In my opinion, He did just that with the introduction of Connie. Because I could verify a lot of her channeling through the equipment, it allowed me to believe even more of what she was getting. This got us to the next point in the journey. Many times throughout this brief history of my life, you will see that I'd hit a point where I didn't know where to go, and I'd ask for help and received it, which led me to another level of

---

[9] To watch *Devil's Tree: Rooted Evil* the movie, it is available on Amazon Prime. DISCLAIMER: This film is Not Rated and has Extreme Violence, Nudity, and Adult Language. Visit www.magicflamefilms.com for more information.

understanding. Plus, the mind can only process so much at one time. I'm sure I was led to the next aspect only when I was ready.

I was extremely excited to learn there was something we could do to help the spirits, but Connie's channeling also posed potential issues that raised serious questions. We had been out with her a couple of times already when she decided one night to share something with us. Something that, for some people, is possibly going be the toughest thing out of all of this to believe. But when finished with the book, there will be no doubt about how the power of what she shared with us that night continues to shape the direction of my life.

After a session in a park known as a mass grave because of the over 80 people killed in the hurricane of 1928, a powerful storm that came onto shore with little to no warning, causing thousands of deaths, Connie shared that the angel she speaks with, known as J., is—get ready—Jesus Christ. Everyone looked at each other with a confused look on their faces, and I didn't know what to say. She very nicely said that she doesn't openly share that but believes the intuitive soft voice she hears is Jesus the Christ. It's interesting because if she'd said this the first time out with her, we probably wouldn't have met up again. If I was reading this book and just got to this part, I might even want to stop reading it. Not because I didn't believe in Jesus—you know I do. But because who is this woman to think SHE is channeling Jesus Christ? And why would Jesus choose to come through this person, who seemed extremely nice and spiritual, but I didn't see the stigmata on her hands or a glowing halo over her head.

I also thought, how easy would it be for some spirit or even worse, some demon to disguise themselves as Jesus and possess this woman to deceive her? Yeah, every kind of question and doubt ran through my mind in that instant. But what I couldn't deny was how she had been correct with most of the channeling, and some of it was easily verified with the evidence we captured. But I just didn't know what to make of this Jesus claim.

There wasn't much said after she told us this, and she was very graceful about it. She didn't seem bothered that we were clearly in disbelief, and she didn't try to convince us. To her, it was just a fact of her life, and whoever chose to believe it could, and whoever didn't, she didn't hold it against them. I found that to be a very refreshing way of handling people's skepticism, but I just got done processing the fact that actual voices could be recorded, and these voices said semi-intelligent things, such as "help me," "get out," "need light," and "I'm stuck." I wasn't ready to accept the idea that Jesus Christ chose to come through a lady living in Palm Beach County.

Nikki definitely wasn't buying into it and expressed her disbelief in Connie later on when we got home that night. Nikki had told me months prior that she was open to the idea of Jesus as a good man who once lived, but as far as Him being the Son of God, she didn't think that to be the case. I respected her beliefs even though I felt He was a little bit more special than just a "good" man. So, when this came out from Connie, Nikki said she'd still go along but would remain skeptical of Connie in general.

Over the next month, we met up with Connie at a few different places, such as a mausoleum, a cemetery, and a park. Connie would check intuitively to see which spirits were there and wanted help. If they wanted to talk, Connie would channel them, and I would counsel them with whatever experience, strength, and hope I could offer. Their stories were always so captivating and unique. Spirits that had anger from losing someone, dying before their time, lack of belief in God, etc. But there was always so much more to their stories, and what we found was that there was always a lesson in their stories for us—holding on to resentments, fear, unfulfilled desires, and so on. I would say whatever it was, I felt inspired to tell them and suggest that they ask for a God of their understanding, or misunderstanding, in most cases.

Towards the end of each session, the spirit, through Connie, would always describe, but in their own way, what they saw when the Light appeared. Sometimes, it was a man that they'd say looked like Jesus. Sometimes, it was a family member, and sometimes it was an angel. But it was always a fantastic feeling, and the best part was I would always capture a couple of responses through the spirit box that would validate these experiences.

But even then, the Jesus thing was still kind of bothering me. What if I'm being deceived by some spirit? What if she's being deceived? *She just couldn't be channeling the real Jesus*, I thought. These concerns arose when she first told us this, and they were starting to resurface again. While we were leaving, I asked Connie if I could ask Jesus a question. She, of course, said yes. I asked Him, "What if I'm having a hard time believing you're really Jesus?" The answer was perfect, in my opinion. He said, "Go home and pray to me, Jesus Christ. Ask me to come to you, and no other power can get in the way of that connection. When you call on my name, it is only I who responds."

He went on to say some other personal things that were meaningful, and when I went home, I thought about all of it some more. I didn't get to this point by basing my spiritual beliefs on what someone else said or did. I had been down a hard path, and establishing some kind of conscious contact with the God of my understanding was something I was proud to be working on, even if I didn't hear Him speak direct words to me like Connie was receiving. But I also couldn't deny multiple channeled messages that were too specific and correct to be flukes, not to mention the audio evidence that backed up a lot of it. I also only ever felt love coming from each message she channeled. So, as "J." had suggested, I prayed to Jesus Christ specifically. Now, I thought of Him often, but I didn't fully understand what it meant to have personal contact with Him.

Since being incarcerated and up to this point, I just prayed to God, the Source of all creation, whatever that meant, and life seemed to work out better. I heard what I perceived to be God (Good Orderly Direction) through the group conscience in the Twelve Step meetings. I saw what I perceived to be Her (Mother Nature) in a sunset. Once in a while, I'd catch a 3:16 on the clock and think of Jesus. All of these things made up my communication with what I believed to be God. But this whole experience was causing me to examine my old relationship with who I thought Jesus to be. Praying to Him that night, I asked for guidance, but I also asked a specific question. I asked Him what His message would be to the atheist. I didn't receive the answer at that moment, but I felt very close to Him. The best way to describe it was an intense and unmistakable feeling of love.

The next time we were set to meet, we decided to visit an area near an old plantation. It was towards the end of September and a perfect time to sit outside in Florida. Not too hot and not as many bugs. I remember my film *Not For Human Consumption* was accepted into the Indie Spirit Film Festival in Colorado, where myself, Nikki, and Chris were going to be traveling to within the next few days. We found some picnic tables under an orange-lit pavilion and set up.

On this particular night, a friend of Connie's named Ron, who was a Palm Beach County Sheriff Deputy, wanted to tag along and see what we were doing. I thought it was cool this decorated officer wanted to investigate the afterlife and not just criminal cases, not to mention with a three-time convicted felon. We welcomed him, and before beginning, Connie asked if J. had any opening message for anyone or the group. These opening messages sometimes were some of the most profound and powerful messages that came from Connie. She immediately connected with J., which only took moments, and began channeling a response. "Josh, the only message I have would be for them to live with love in their hearts. If they do this, they've accepted Me without knowing it."

I couldn't believe what I was hearing. Not only was the response amazing, it was the perfect answer to the question I had asked in prayer that night alone. How could this be? The rest of the group seemed confused as they never heard me ask a question. He then said something else, "You will have a big surprise waiting for you in Colorado." That was all He said, and I didn't dare ask Him to elaborate. But the fact that He answered my question was another piece in helping me believe.

We began the session, and it was apparent right away that a deceased slave owner was coming through. In what was one of the most interesting and powerful sessions we've done early on, we listened as this man described what he interpreted as going to hell.[10]

The next day, it was time to pack up and prepare to fly to Colorado for the film festival. I couldn't stop thinking about what this "big surprise" could be. I was grateful because after the film would premiere in Colorado, it was set to open in select theaters in Miami and L.A. It was all very exciting. When we were in Colorado, I figured we'd have time to sneak away to a cemetery and try and help some souls. If we ran into any communication

---

[10] Watch this video at HOPEparanormal.com/video Video #1. Videos can also be seen at YouTube.com/HopeParanormalWhiteLight under "Book Playlist"

troubles, we'd call Connie on speaker and see if she could remotely connect to the spirits present where we were. We had no idea if it would work, but it was worth a try.

When we arrived in Colorado, one of the festival representatives was there to greet us with a car and take us to the hotel. It was amazing, everyone was so nice, and with over 100 films showing, they were excited to have us there. We flew in on a Friday, and the film was premiering that Sunday, so we had a couple of days to enjoy the events, parties, and workshops. We got to know other filmmakers and discussed our passion for making motion pictures.

That Saturday, the three of us headed over to Fairlawn Cemetery in Colorado Springs and found a spot on a grassy hill to set up. It was very cold, and I remember Nikki not wanting to get out of the car. I don't blame her; I don't handle the cold well either. But we were there to hear the voices that weren't being heard anymore—to help the forgotten ones. I set up the spirit box and pulled out my phone, and gave Connie a call. I put her on speaker and asked her to connect to the spirits around us. I had no idea if this would work, but before I could question it, she was picking up on a woman. This woman stated she owned the land and didn't want other spirits to leave it. It was an interesting session[11], and after conversing with the woman, we felt we could help in some way. What I do know is that we again captured responses through the box that validated parts of what Connie was getting. It showed that someone didn't have to be physically in the presence of the spirit to connect with them. It was all so fascinating, and we were just scratching the surface.

Sunday came, and it was time for the film to premiere; the theatre was packed. Just seeing it on the big screen at that

---

[11] Watch this video at HOPEparanormal.com/video Video #2.

moment, all the hard work that went into making this film felt completely worth it. Afterward, it received a roaring applause, and Chris and I just looked at each other, feeling proud of what we had accomplished. After all the other films finished showing, it was time for the Awards Ceremony. Over the last few days, we had seen some excellent films shown, met some fantastic people and had such an amazing time—what more could we have asked for? All of a sudden, the category for "BEST Feature Film was announced, and we were nominated; we couldn't believe it. Out of almost 1,000 submissions, only 100 films were accepted, and we were nominated to win the Festival. Well, all I was thinking was it was an honor just to be nominated, but then the host opened the envelope.

"And the award for Best Film goes to… *Not For Human Consumption.*"

Chris and I both jumped up and screamed. "We won, we won!" What a perfect end to such a memorable weekend.

Right then, it hit me; this was the "big surprise" we had awaiting us in Colorado. I never expected to win and was in total shock. It was then I knew there was something very special happening. A Power, calling himself Jesus, had now given us message after message through Connie that had all been correct, each filled with positivity and love. We left Colorado with the award for "Best Film," a lot of new friends, and yet again, another spiritual experience that revealed something greater was at work.

When we got home from Colorado, I was so excited to share the news of the win with Connie. She was so happy for us and just blown away that was the surprise J. was talking about. Most of the time, she would channel messages and not even remember what was said after. I asked her why she thought this was the case, and her feeling was she was channeling from a different part of her brain, and it wasn't being processed the same way a normal conversation would. I would joke with her and say, if I could talk to Jesus, I'd ask him everything, even driving directions. She would laugh and say it doesn't work that way. I still couldn't understand what she meant.

We were looking forward to getting back out to one of our regular locations and do a session. While on the phone with Connie beforehand, trying to coordinate a time to meet, I asked her if J. had any suggestion about which place to go. We particularly didn't need to be told where to go, and when I did occasionally ask, I was given the answer to "go where we felt guided." But this time she got quiet after asking and then said, "This can't be right, and if it is, I don't feel comfortable doing the session tonight." I had never heard her talk like that, and I needed to know what she was told. She went on to tell me that J. calmly mentioned to her the devil would be present on this particular night, that he didn't want us helping a specific group of spirits. I asked why, and she elaborated that this group was bad and had inspired many horrible acts from the other side affecting this dimension. But there was a small window of opportunity in being able to help free them from evil bondage.

Well, this put a damper on the positive feeling I had been experiencing up to this point. What was this woman channeling? Was the devil now going to come? I mean, are we even sure the devil exists in the traditional sense as Lucifer, a fallen angel, who rules the underworld? After my demonic experience that night early on in prison, my thoughts wavered on whether there was an actual "devil" out there as opposed to a legion of demons creating havoc instead. Regardless of what I believed, when I told Nikki about what Connie had just shared with me, she decided she wouldn't go. I, of course, was still intrigued and felt compelled to go.

Visiting Connie from Denmark around this time were friends of hers named Mette and Bent. They were two of the kindest, most intelligent people I had ever met. Bent was a psychologist and had expressed a real interest in coming along with us to sit in while doing one of our sessions. Mette, a former school teacher, had joined us during the Devil's Tree session, and it only seemed fitting Bent would accompany us this time when the devil himself was supposed to be there. And who better than a psychologist to help counter the cunning and manipulative ways of the prince of darkness?

Again, I share these stories with you because it's what happened. In the books I've read in the past on specific subjects, most of the authors have done their research. Some of them cite references to back up what they write about, and some have had personal experiences they share with compelling details. But unless you believe them on their word, they are just stories. With most of what I share with you in this book, there is a video to go along with the account. Early on in this journey, my ability to record and log evidence wasn't as good as it is today. But with each video, there are at least two to three pieces of evidence that back up these stories. I am so grateful that without realizing how important these videos would be, I started to record these crazy things from the beginning.[12]

So, there we were, the three of us, Connie, Bent, and myself, sitting on a bench in Flamingo Park. I had my spirit box out, and with Bent quietly sitting there observing like Dr. Sigmund Freud, Connie checked in with J. Immediately, we were told the spirits mentioned earlier were present along with two other groups that

---

needed help. I asked if the "fallen one" was there, and we were told no, not yet.

There was a group of benign spirits that asked for prayers and, from what we were able to understand, moved on pretty quickly. Then it was time for this so-called "bad" group of spirits we were told about. They had caused bad things to happen to people and were supposedly trapped by the devil, forcing them out of "sheer terror" to continue to do his so-called bidding. When Connie began channeling one of these bad spirits to find out more, the spirit expressed fear for even talking to us. Connie then heard J. tell her that the devil was there, watching in the corner. All of our minds raced to try and picture what that might have looked like. Connie seemed uneasy, Bent was calm, and I personally still didn't know what to think.

All of a sudden, Connie gasped, and my camera shut off, which was something that had never happened in the past. There was plenty of battery left, and my finger was nowhere near the power button. I immediately turned it back on and asked Connie what happened. She was pale and seemed shaken. She told us, as quietly and as calmly as anyone could ever say it, that a voice that she instinctively knew somehow was evil, whispered in her ear, "Tonight, when you lay your head down and close your eyes, you're mine." This was very strange, and whether it was the actual devil or not, something said that to her, and she was visibly disturbed.

I asked Connie to ask J. if there was any truth to what was just whispered to her. Without thinking, Connie asked, and from her mouth, almost in a different tone, the words "Absolutely not!" came forth. I don't know what it was, but I'll never forget how those words sounded and felt when they came out of her mouth. Somehow we all just knew and felt the absolute truth in those words. It was like we initially felt fear, and then our faith was reinforced. We finished helping the group, said a prayer, and ended the session. Connie never heard that voice again.[13]

Afterward, discussing what had just happened amongst the three of us, Connie felt J. had some additional things that needed to be said. We were told we did a good job helping the spirits that night, and we were thanked for our compassion. We were also told that we are fully protected by the Light of God, and we never needed to fear evil. That it was the fear that makes us vulnerable, and by keeping our attention on God, evil would never have a chance. Those words resonated as absolute truth for me. I thanked Him and asked what else we could do to help. We were told to learn meditation, pray, and trust in God and that we are being guided. He then stated that I was personally so close to Him that I couldn't separate myself if I wanted to and that I would continue to help people here and in the hereafter.

One of the first questions I asked J. through Connie early on was about Steve Huff's afterlife research, and I received an answer that his work was very important. On this particular night that I was being given these messages, I was also told I would work with Steve very closely on spirit communication in the future and that I would write a book reaching many.

All of this seemed like a lot, and I didn't know what to say. It was all so hard to believe. There was always this little voice, saying, "Josh, you know this is all bullshit, right?" Fear of being taken for a ride, but I had seen how premonitions foretold by Connie came to fruition. In addition to that, many times, I'd hear responses through the box saying the same things she was channeling. By now, you've read that line a few times, but that's how the process worked. We were told something, I wouldn't

---

[13] Watch this video at HOPEparanormal.com/video Video #4.

believe it, and something undeniable would happen, proving it was real. I'd accept it, and then the process would start all over again with something else. But how many times would this need to happen for me to fully believe?

Regardless of what I thought, all of what was said sounded exciting. There was an acronym in Twelve Step recovery meetings known as H.O.W. (Honesty, Open-mindedness, and Willingness). My intentions for doing this were *honest*, and I was *willing* to keep seeking answers; I just needed to keep an *open mind*. But then Connie went and channeled another unbelievable message from J., but this time about Nikki. Just as casually as Connie had given powerful messages in the past, she opened her mouth and began speaking, "Soon Nikki will be given the ability to channel spirit as Connie does."

"What!? I exclaimed. "I'm sorry, what do you mean Nikki is going to channel?"

"Yes, Josh. In one month, she will be able to communicate intuitively with spirits," J. answered.

Just as I was starting to maybe accept the possibility of the wild premonitions I was told moments ago, I now have to digest yet another crazy foretelling. I really didn't know what to say, but my silence and stunned face would be enough to express my shock. Connie said that in all the years of giving readings, she had never given such a message and was pretty surprised herself. I always found it amusing when she would have a conversation with J. She would ask a question and then start getting the answer, and it always sounded like someone else speaking even though it was all coming out of her mouth.

"Jesus, you mean Nikki is going to be able to speak to spirits as I do?" she asked.

"Yes, Connie, but she will see, feel, and hear them," J. said through her.

This was slightly different from how Connie's ability worked as she only heard the spirits' voices. But it was word for word verbatim most times. J. explained that Nikki, in addition to being able to hear, would be clairvoyant (see) as well as clairsentient (feel). As Bent sat there listening to all of this, I wanted to ask him if I could lie down on the bench and pay for a therapy session. I felt like I was going crazy.

Of course, when I got home, I shared with Nikki what happened during the session, the messages J. had given me, and more importantly, the news that she would become an intuitive in a month or so. I saw that it caught her attention and kind of intrigued her, but she ultimately didn't believe it. Who would?

I was struggling with all of this, and I felt like I would have to figure it out all by myself. Nikki had seriously resigned from giving it any more thought, I couldn't ask Connie for more clarity as she was giving us these messages, and if I dared to share this with anyone else, I would surely be committed. Regardless, I still felt compelled to keep exploring all of it. I remember Connie, Mette, and myself still meeting once a week and helping spirits cross over. I'd record the sessions with my camera, where afterward I'd go home, review the footage, and caption the responses. I'd then upload the video to the H.O.P.E. Paranormal channel that had about 500 loyal subscribers watching and commenting with their thoughts. Most found Connie's channeling informative, authentic, and captivating, and when people heard a response or two through the spirit box verifying what she was saying, they too would see the significance in the evidence.

THE GIFTS

It was the middle of December 2013, and it had been well over a month from when Connie first gave the message that Nikki would receive her intuitive ability. Needless to say, Nikki still wasn't hearing or seeing any spirits and this only fueled her contempt for Connie's messages even more. In fact, it had gotten to the point where Nikki didn't want me to go out and meet with Connie and the others anymore, and if I wasn't a man strong in his convictions, I might have listened. I wasn't disrespectful to my partner, but I wasn't ready to subscribe to Nikki's line of thinking, not just yet. As unbelievable as all of this was, there were just too many "coincidences" and too much evidence to ignore. I still needed to find out the truth if it was possible.

One day, before one of our crossover sessions, Connie and I met up for coffee. Even though Connie was the one channeling, I found at times she was genuinely surprised and blown away with what was coming through. Sitting over a cup of coffee, I asked to speak to Jesus. I told her I wanted to ask Him more about His life, what else He did that wasn't well known. Before I knew it, Connie had tuned in to J. and was already giving me a reply that He was willing to speak. I mentioned the widely known fact that Jesus, the man, was a carpenter or a craftsman and asked what it was that He made with His hands when He was alive. What I didn't know at the time asking that innocent inquiry was that it would reveal something so powerful, so profound that lives are still being touched by it to this day. It was in subtle moments like these that some of the most impactful spiritual experiences happened.

When I asked the question, Connie brought forth the answer straight from J. just as she always did.

"I made tables and chairs as well as the yokes for the oxen. I made many other pieces for practical use. I also made keepsakes for people."

Upon hearing this, I mentioned that I had attended both Sunday and Catholic schools my whole life—I was even an altar boy—yet I had never heard of Jesus making any type of keepsakes for people. I asked what these keepsakes were. He told me they were little pieces of wood that had a design carved into them. I asked what the design was. He went on to say the design held His entire Word and encapsulated all of His teachings. Connie stopped channeling for a moment to clarify what it was she was hearing, which was always a strange thing to witness. We were just both so intrigued with what was being said. She received confirmation through His words that, yes, she was hearing Him correctly.

I asked if He would explain or show us the design, and again, the childlike question received a "yes" as an answer. I had only ever seen Connie channel verbally, but per J.'s instructions, Connie took a pen and a scrap piece of paper and began to roughly draw a design. I asked her how she was doing this, and she answered, her hand was being guided. Of course, I was suspicious of this as that's just my nature, but there was no time to allow my skepticism to get in the way of what was turning out to be a very interesting experience. As Connie began to draw a circle, I wondered, could this woman have been sitting on this design in her head, ready to release it when the time was right? What now am I going to have to process here as another "hard to believe" moment approaches?

As she finished drawing the circle, she put a dot in the middle with lines running away from it. Connie expressed that this had happened only one other time where her hand was guided by spirit, but nothing like this. Once the lines were drawn, there were a total of 14 that fanned out from the middle dot to the inner edge of the circle, even extending past a little bit. It looked like a wheel of some sort. The design seemed simple enough, but what did it mean?

Connie then continued to write while receiving the information. In addition to the design, there were specific words that went along with it. Over the middle dot, she wrote the word "God." In each triangle section inside the circle, she wrote a different word: "Love, "Peace, "Stillness, "Joy, "Trust, "Giving, "Compassion, "Gratitude," "Security," "Honesty," "Truth," "Fullness," "Wisdom," and "Salvation." On the outside of the circle, where each of the 14 points met the edge, she wrote another 14 words: "Fear," "Lust," "Anger," "Pain," "Sorrow," "Envy," "Malice," "Need," "Disillusionment," "Self-deceit," "Betrayal," "Dishonesty," "Insecurity," and "Separation."

Connie then put the pen down and asked J. what it all meant. Immediately, she received an answer.

"A person has fourteen inner qualities and fourteen outer qualities. The dot in the middle is the "Source," which is God. The lines that run away represent fear. That fear brings a person to their outer qualities and has them going round and round in the outer ring. What eventually brings someone back to God is their inner qualities."[14]

I looked at Connie with amazement; she was equally shocked. I asked Him how this design came about. He continued, "One day, I was sharing my teachings with someone, the entirety and simplicity of it all. The young man picked up a stick and started drawing in the sand, trying to grasp what it was I was sharing with him. I then gently guided his hand, completing the design making it a perfect depiction of my Word in more ways than one.

---

[14] See the design in chapter *The Life Piece*. page 173.

Together we would carve the design into little round pieces of wood and give them to people to have, as a reminder."

Absolutely blown away by the information and story I was just told, I asked what they were called. He said they didn't have a name but that we could call them Life Pieces if we wanted to.

Connie and I were like two students sitting there, listening to a wise teacher share the meaning of life. Aside from amazement, I still needed to try and stay grounded here. I either witnessed her A) keep this incredibly powerful and meaningful design secret until someone like me, a motivated seeker, came along for her to put on this amazing performance, or B) just channel the consciousness of an ascended Master who gave us a very special, lost treasure. All I knew was that story and design had struck a deep chord within me.

Sitting outside of this coffee shop, we were there for so long discussing what just happened, we didn't get a chance to conduct our session. I immediately went home and started rummaging through my garage for spare scraps of wood. I found a small block and my old whittling kit from when I was a kid. There, in my garage, I sat and carved this piece of wood into the exact shape and design drawn on the diagram. I then drilled a hole in the middle at the top and carefully carved lines down the sides. When I was done, in my hand, I held the Life Piece. There was power in it; I felt it. Regardless of where or who it came from, it felt special and was clearly meaningful.

Connie and I would later register the design in hopes of one day being able to share it with as many people as possible. But in the meantime, with Christmas just around the corner, I decided to carve a few for family and close friends as gifts. I ordered blocks of olive wood from Jerusalem, pruned from trees over two thousand years old. Like an elf, I got to work whittling away in my garage, making close to twenty Life Pieces in less than two weeks.

Every year in the past, I'd scramble to the malls and scour Amazon for gifts and always felt like I came up short in the "sentimental" department. The holidays were always such a stressful time, and this was the first Christmas in a while that it didn't feel that way. The only other time I can remember it was like that was the first year I got out of prison. I had no money, and the only gifts I could give to my family were hand-sewn stuffed bears, like the ones I made in prison for Toys for Tots. There's something special about making the gifts yourself for the people you love. And what more could someone ask for on Christmas than a hand-carved, channeled gift from Christ that inspired people to remember what was important in life? Needless to say, I was excited to give gifts that year.

Christmas Eve, I arrived home from my office after receiving a disturbing call from a friend of mine. He had shared with me his fourteen-year-old son had committed suicide by hanging himself in his closet with a belt. I was devastated for him and tried my best to offer my condolences, but what can you say in a situation like that? Your heart just goes out to the family, and you hope they're able to recover from such a tragedy. As I pulled into my garage, I saw Nikki sitting in one of the two chairs we sat in each night while watching the sun set. Visibly disturbed from the news that was just shared with me, I didn't get much out when telling Nikki before she cut me off, motioning me not to say another word. With no hesitation, she blurts out that his son did it in a closet with a belt. We both just looked at each other stunned.

"How did you know that?" I asked.

"I don't know," she quickly answered.

She went on to tell me that she started to feel weird during the day and when I just mentioned my friend's son, that she got a flash of this young boy in a closet with a brown belt around his neck. I couldn't believe it. There was absolutely no way for her to know that. Was this the gift Connie had foretold? On Christmas Eve of all nights? Nikki, still not understanding what she was feeling, told me to ask for someone deceased that only I would know. There were a few I could've asked about, but it was my friend Adam that had died just two years prior. I wanted to ask about him.

Adam's story is long, so I'll just give you the reader's digest version. He was someone I cared very much about. He was a newcomer at Twelve Step meetings and asked if he could start attending with me. Of course, I agreed, and he met me every day for six months. He started getting better and better until one day, he relapsed. Stealing a watch and an iPod from my house when he was under the influence, I got upset. We had a huge fight, and he stormed out. A few weeks later, the home invasion happened, and I thought he might have had something to do with it. When I hired the private investigators, I gave them his information to check out. What I didn't realize was that argument we had would be the last time I'd ever see him. Murdered in the streets of Miami trying to buy drugs, Adam died a horrible death and had nothing to do with my robbery. I missed him very much and partly blamed myself for what happened to him.

When I asked Nikki to see if she could get anything, she immediately picked up on his appearance and demeanor. He was tall, thin, and kind of had a youthful swagger to him. I asked if there was anything she could hear him say, and after a moment of intently listening, she let out an exaggerated, "What's up, man!" As general as that sounds, this was exactly how he used to greet me. Of course, the ultimate skeptic in me needed real proof, and as interesting as this was, it didn't prove anything just yet. But she was right about my friend's son's suicide, and there was no way for her to know that. She was correct about how Adam looked, how he acted, and what he used to say. Not to mention it was foretold that Nikki would receive this ability. Why was this so hard for me to accept?

I'll tell you why, because it's crazy. It's insane. It challenges every bit of logic and reasoning in the human mind, and we don't want to feel insane. I had such a hard time accepting that Connie was a real channeler, and it took quite a few sessions with strong evidence for me to believe—the atheist question answered by J., the Colorado Film Festival win, the channeling of the Life Piece, and verifiable messages from spirits with audio evidence confirming what she was getting.

I asked Nikki questions about Adam's death, and her answers were correct. Things only I knew, how exactly it happened and where the killer was caught driving Adam's car. But soon, she felt Adam didn't want to discuss his death anymore. She felt he was still upset about it. I asked why he hadn't crossed over, and this was yet another topic he didn't want to discuss. I was used to the way Connie channeled but this was different yet still very effective. When someone you know very well sends you an email or text message, even though you can't hear their voice, by the way they write or what they say, you can still tell if it's them or not. It felt the same way here. Nikki would just say what she felt or heard, and at times, it may not have been much, but it was the right answer using the same verbiage Adam would use. One of the things Adam told her was that he stays with his mom a lot but wanted to hang out with us. It was like another level of communication we were experiencing.

In the past, we knew spirits were around, but at that moment, the energy and what Nikki was getting made it feel like my friend was right there hanging out with us in our garage. The fact that I knew Nikki, that she wasn't just some woman I met, that she was receiving correct information out of thin air, was blowing both of our minds.

After that, we saw Eva on the baby monitor waking from her nap. This new psychic ability would have to wait until later when Eva went to bed for the night. But my head was swimming. *How crazy was this?* I thought. I started thinking of people I'd ask to come through later on. The thing was, Nikki felt tired and very hungry afterwards, like a lot of her energy was used when she was in that intuitive space.

Once dinner was done, we spent some time with our daughter and then put her to bed so we could wrap presents. Eva's gifts were carefully placed under the tree, along with my modestly wrapped Life Pieces. I was so excited, it was Eva's second Christmas, and we had family and close friends coming over after Eva opened gifts in the morning. To be honest, I was more excited about Nikki's newly discovered gift, but I assumed she was still tired from earlier. But without asking her, she informed me she got a second wind and wanted me to ask for more people. She was truly excited, and it seemed that however doubtful she was about Connie and her messages in the past, it was no longer an issue.

What Nikki picked up intuitively already with my friend's son and Adam was impressive. This time I was going to ask for my aunt Roseanne who had passed in 2009 from cancer. She was my godmother, and I loved her very much. Nikki knew I had an aunt that passed away, but I didn't discuss her very often. She was a very strong-willed woman, and before she died, she and I had a short period we didn't talk. On her deathbed, I got to make amends for my behavior and tell her I loved her. As she lay there, her body riddled with cancer, she grabbed my hand and said, "It doesn't matter, Josh, I love you. I'm going home." My sister, mom, uncle, and I cried for a bit, and then she was gone. I had thought about reaching out to her in the afterlife but never tried.

So there we were, back in our chairs but this time wearing our pajamas. Nikki asked me who I wanted to talk to, and I said my aunt Roseanne. Nikki sat there a moment staring at nothing just as Connie would while connecting with spirit. A second or two passed, and she sensed a woman. I asked if it was Roseanne and Nikki said she didn't know but that maybe I should ask something, anything. Instead of asking something ridiculous like "Aunt Ro, is that you?" I wanted to ask something that would verify it was her right away. But before I could come up with the right question, Nikki said she felt this woman being somewhat cold to her. I asked her why she felt that way, and Nikki said she could see the woman standing there looking at me but not wanting to look at Nikki. "You can see this?" I asked.

She went on to tell me my aunt stated she disapproved of what we were doing, talking to spirits. I couldn't believe what I was hearing for two reasons. One, that this is exactly the way my aunt thought when she was alive. She was raised Catholic, and this kind of thing is frowned upon by those that don't understand it. After my Ouija experience, she was so upset with me, telling me I needed to get to church to be blessed by a priest. Of course, Nikki never knew about this, and it makes it that much more interesting. The other reason this was so crazy to me was the fact that she was on the other side, as a spirit crossed over, and yet she still thought this was something we shouldn't be doing.

Nikki then told me my aunt said she loved me very much and that would never change. Even though I can't remember everything that was said that night word for word, I remember everything Nikki got was correct. Almost as if she was incapable of being wrong. I'd ask a question and the right answer, or a part of it would come forth. It was quite remarkable to witness, and for me, it was miraculous. Strange and baffling, but miraculous. I thought to myself, *I wonder if she could talk to Jesus like Connie does.*

He was the one that said through Connie that this would happen. I shared my thoughts with Nikki, and she said she wasn't ready to ask for Him. I asked why she felt that way, and she said this was a lot to process, that she just wasn't ready yet. I completely understood as I was trying to process all of this myself. We went to bed, and I must have laid there for an hour in prayer, just talking to God, sharing with Him how I felt and how grateful I was for this experience.

Christmas morning, we woke up early, got Eva out of bed, and opened gifts. We watched the *Christmas Story* marathon on TV while we entertained family and friends throughout the day. With each person I gave the Life Piece to, I shared a little of the story but mainly focused on what it meant. I figured there would be those that wouldn't necessarily see the significance or believe how it came about, but I didn't care. I had made these pieces for people because I loved them. My father, always supportive and intrigued with what I was doing, accepted his gift, and handled it carefully. He wasn't at all religious but had started to open up more to the idea of God in recent years. My mom, a spiritual woman but more traditional in her beliefs, was gracious but skeptical it came from Christ, and who could blame her? My close friends, the ones who had seen some of the videos and work we were doing, were very excited to receive these spiritual keepsakes as J. called them.

Later that night, after all the loved ones had gone home, Nikki and I were in our chairs. She knew that I wanted to see what would happen if she tried connecting to Jesus. She was still unsure about asking for Him for whatever reason, and as I stated, I respected her feelings. But as we were even discussing it, something happened. Nikki looked at me and then said, "Actually, I think He's here." I, of course, asked why she felt that way, and she described a feeling of just knowing He was there. Then from her mouth came, "Hello Josh, it is I." I was in disbelief and asked how this was possible. I was told that through Him, anything was possible. I then asked if I'd ever believe in this fully. Very bluntly but lovingly, Nikki channeled the answer, "Josh, your faith will be handed to you on a silver platter." I didn't know what that meant, but I liked the sound of it.

With my head again swimming with a million thoughts and questions, I asked the only thing I could think to ask at the moment. The answer I received might have been one of, if not the most powerful response I've ever heard channeled. I asked, almost stuttering over my words, "What are we to take away from an experience like this?" Nikki looked at me with an almost confused look on her face, and with a "matter-of-fact" tone said, *Look what I did to the non-believer.*

Wow!

In that moment, just like with the few times I had felt it with Connie, I wasn't hearing Nikki; I was hearing Jesus Christ somehow. When Nikki channeled that answer, we both looked at each other with a look of complete awe. I don't know how else to describe it. Just less than a year ago, she was in a place where she didn't even know if Jesus ever existed, and now she was channeling a form of His consciousness. That answer He gave held real power just in those few words. I asked about Connie, and even though Nikki would've told you that she wasn't as convinced of Connie's messages as I was, through Nikki, J. confirmed Connie's channeling. This was interesting to hear come directly from Nikki.

One thing I wanted to ask about was a reoccurring message Connie had been getting every once in a while during sessions. While channeling J., she would bring up this topic about starting a community in Alaska, and it would always come out at random times. She would share that starting a spiritual community in the mountains somewhere was her dream and that Nikki and I were invited to be a part of it if we wanted. It sounded like a cool idea, but I had no desire to live in Alaska. When she'd ask J. about it, His answers were always vague but supportive. I had expressed that I wouldn't move to Alaska anytime soon, that there was enough to process for a lifetime with all that's happened. But internally, I had decided that if somehow something like that was to come about, I'd at least go check it out.

When I asked Jesus about this through Nikki, I was told that we wouldn't be going to Alaska. I asked why this was something that came out in Connie's channeling sometimes. He proceeded to tell me, Connie desires to be in a spiritual community somewhere in the mountains, which there's nothing wrong with. Someone picking up on an intuitive message isn't necessarily receiving it 100% clearly most of the time. If the person takes care of themselves by meditating, communing with a Higher Power, lives morally right, and checks their ego often, the information they receive from spirit will be the most accurate it can be. He goes on to explain that living in this material world, we have desires that cause attachments. It's okay to have desires; we just can't be attached to them. Being in Alaska for Connie was a desire she was still attached to, and sometimes it would bleed into J.'s true message. He was explaining to us through Nikki, which was taking some getting used to, that this was something that can happen and the only way to prevent this is through constant, honest self-appraisal. It was such a remarkable lesson to learn.

He then explained that soon He was going to gently tell Connie that she wouldn't be going to Alaska. I knew that would be something that would upset her and asked how He would do that, surely not through Nikki. Here I am questioning Christ on His plan, to make sure it's a good one, you know, 'cause I'm sure He needs help, right? *Ha.* In a loving way, I was told to leave that up to Him. What I found to be absolutely amazing was here we had a certain persona, a consciousness said to be Jesus Christ, and He spoke through both women with the same tone and demeanor. It was like talking to the same person through two different telephones. What happened next was a very pivotal moment in proving the legitimacy of the messages coming from both women.

It was January 16th, 2014, a few weeks after Nikki had received her ability on Christmas Eve. We hadn't seen Connie since before the holiday, and with New Year's, it had been more difficult. But on this particular night, I was able to get us all together for a session. I also invited Ron, the Sheriff, along with a good friend of mine, Ken, to join in.

Sitting outside near a mausoleum on the island of Palm Beach, we all gathered around Connie as she was about to begin. Now that Nikki was able to channel as well, she agreed to try and connect to the spirits once Connie was done. Ron was a big fan of asking before the sessions if J. had an open message for anyone. I was more on the side that if J. wanted to say something to any of us, He would. Ron asked the question, and Connie readied herself to receive the message. She began as she always did, staring off into a void, and then the words came out, "Connie, tonight I have a message for you."

Surprised, Connie replied, "Oh, okay. You normally don't have a message for me. What could this be?" I watched intently, wondering, could this be what Jesus was talking about to the both of us the other night? Connie then began channeling J.'s message, "Connie, I want to tell you that now is not the time you will be going to the mountains." Connie, a little embarrassed and taken aback at what she was just told through her own mouth, looked over at me and half-jokingly said, "This is because you didn't want to go to Alaska, Josh, isn't it?" Flabbergasted and taken aback myself, I stayed quiet. Connie wasn't really mad at me, but I could tell this message from J. caught her off guard.

She then went back to receiving the rest of the message. "Connie, I know you would like to go, and someday you may, but not now. There is still more work to be done with each of you in different lengths of time." Connie gracefully accepted the message and stated that she would discuss the rest when she got home. She then asked if there was another message for anyone else but was told not at that time. She then joked, "So, I'm the only lucky one tonight?" After, we proceeded to do the crossover session, praying for any spirits wanting help. This was the night I recorded one of the brightest orbs I've ever captured on video.[15]

Driving home, Nikki and I were just sort of stunned. I was for several reasons. What a mind-blowing experience. How could anyone explain what just happened without considering that this could be exactly what we've been told it is, a metaphysical, spiritual, and Divine experience? Just to recap a few of the main points to remember. Connie comes along and says she channels Jesus. I pray to Jesus on my own and ask a specific question, and

---

[15] Watch this clip at HOPEparanormal.com/video Video #5.

the answer is given to me through Connie's channeling the next day. Then Nikki is told she would be able to communicate with the same Consciousness in time. That time comes, and she is "made a believer" with her own ability by receiving accurate intuitive messages. Nikki and I are then told by J. that He will deliver the message to Connie directly regarding not going to the Alaskan mountains. The next time we see Connie, spoken directly from her own mouth, in front of many witnesses, J. tells her exactly what we were told in the privacy of our garage a few nights earlier.

Why was that message delivered in public and not in the privacy of Connie's home just to her? My thoughts are for a couple of reasons. One, because Connie felt very attached to that desire to go to the mountains, she might not have accepted the message if she heard it by herself. Witnesses were needed. Of course, the message could have come through Nikki, but Connie wouldn't have believed it if it did. The second reason, Nikki and I needed to hear that message delivered in person. It would prove Nikki was connecting with the same Consciousness as Connie. Plus, seeing it happen this way would make it hard for me to discount the experience later on.

THE FIRST APPEARANCE

A couple of nights after meeting with Connie, Nikki and I decided to sit in our garage and conduct a quick session, or so we thought. My film was slated for a theatrical release at the beginning of February 2014 as the Colorado and California Festival wins got us enough attention for our limited national release in Los Angeles and Miami. This means I was getting busier, but I didn't want to put what we were doing in the paranormal field on hold in any way.

Sitting in the garage, we would pick a location elsewhere, and Nikki would practice a form of remote viewing by connecting with the spirits there. Even though we weren't physically at the location, we felt we could effectively help in different places. We had seen Connie, as well as others, do this, sometimes describing great detail about the location with undeniable accuracy. At the time, my friend, Chris, lived in a small apartment not too far from us, and I thought it would be a good idea to see if Nikki could connect to any of the spirits over there. Again, I feel the need to reiterate that we never would've made it this far down the path without witnessing certain happenings that validated these claims. With each instance, there were many factors that made it intriguing, but there was always at least one undeniable fact that made it impossible to discount the experience.

So, Nikki connects to Chris's residence. Quickly, she sees five spirits in a small field next to his house. She had never been there before, so whatever she was receiving as far as the layout of the landscape wasn't from memory. Near the tree line, she faintly saw some animal, with a few of them hiding behind the trees. She said she could see they were able to stand upright and had horns on their heads. I asked if they were some kind of entity, and she replied with the word "retrievers." She said it just popped into her mind. I wondered, *Retrievers of what, souls?* As quickly as she noticed these things, her face dropped and instantly became the most surprised I had ever seen her. "What is it? What do you see?" I asked excitedly. One word exited her mouth, "Jesus."

She proceeded to explain that a man resembling what she believed Jesus to look like walked illuminated across the field over to the five spirits. As He walked, she explained the retrievers snarled and hid even deeper in the trees. As Jesus approached the spirits, He touched them one by one, resulting in each of them disappearing. In their place, a small yellow flower appeared on the

72

ground. I remember listening to Nikki describe this scene just as a child would describe an exciting moment in their favorite movie. It was so real for her, she had genuine excitement in seeing this play out, and I was hanging on her every word.

She then asked J. why He chose that moment to appear to her. The answer He gave her was a beautiful one. He didn't want the last thing for her to see that night to be the faces of those creatures, a low vibrational entity that feeds off fear. Instead, she would remember Him always and even suggested I draw an illustration of what she described. He also told us to ask Chris to check the field in the morning, that there would be five small yellow flowers alone. That these flowers were there because of what just happened, He explained.

At that moment, I got this vision of a red-haired woman, wearing white, smiling at us. I immediately shared the vision with Nikki, and she again got excited.

"I just saw her as well, her name is Alma, and she's this kind soul who's been appearing to me," Nikki explained.

"How was it that I saw her as well?" I asked.

"You just received your first vision, Josh," Jesus said through Nikki. Immediately I knew I was receiving the intuitive gift myself in some capacity. Like Ralphie in the movie *Christmas Story*, when he finally receives his Red Rider BB Gun on Christmas morning, I was elated. I couldn't think of anything more special than to be able to see and communicate with spirits, ultimately deepening my connection to God.

To clarify, I asked what that statement "first vision" meant. Just as I had thought, Nikki received more communication detailing how in a couple of weeks' time, similar to what she was told by Connie, I would receive the ability to see, feel, and hear spirit myself. Was this what He meant when I was told my faith "would be handed to me on a silver platter?" But before I could even contemplate that statement, I was also told that for me to receive the gift, I would have to go through a purge of some kind. I knew what the term meant, to push out, to get rid of, but what was I being purged of? I was given the answer, ego.

I was told that night, sitting in my garage, that I would be using this ability to help people, that it would be a big part of my life from here on out, and that I would have many spiritual experiences involving this communication. But for that to happen, I would need to keep working on myself, losing more and more of my ego as I progressed. To me, I had done so much work, I thought. Therapy, the Twelve Steps, service work with others, what ego could there be left? Hahahaha, I just laugh when I remember thinking this back then.

All I'll say is, the ego, an entity of itself, which is basically our established identity, the soul identifying with the body, is very tricky. It is not something we slay once in our lifetime and then we are automatically a saint. No, there are many layers to the onion, so to speak. We may think we've let go of "this," and then "that" shows up. It's lifelong work, looking at the self. The ego is something that feels it has to protect us. Protect us from failing, looking stupid, and ultimately not getting what we want in life. What we don't realize is the ego operates on fear-based thoughts. Fear of losing something we have, or fear of not getting something we want. So, really, the results that come from the actions of ego-based thoughts never turn out the way we want.

The way it was explained to me, channeled through Nikki, someone who had never broached any of these topics before in her life, was that we were all given "free will." That meant we were free to do whatever we wanted, but there would be consequences for our actions, which is karma. Anytime we exercised our free will, it was normally to gain something for ourselves. This meant free will usually resulted in someone getting hurt. Either ourselves or someone else, and that could mean emotionally or on a physical level. Now, every time we did something selfless, kind, or loving, it was Divinely inspired.

When I heard this, I couldn't accept it. This meant every idea of mine would ultimately hurt me or someone else, but that any positive thought I had that led to a selfless act was God. The way I took this was, I was incapable of doing good on my own. But Jesus explained it wasn't like that. Everyone has the Creator in them. We either choose to act from the ego-self or allow the God-self in us to come out. This is why in the Twelve Steps, Step 3 is: – "made a decision to turn our *will* and life over to the care of God as we understood Him." It all started to make sense to me.

We were both given a lot that night. The experience of Jesus in the field, my first true psychic vision, not to mention quite a bit of life knowledge that neither of us truly knew. Before going in for the night, I sent Chris a text that he'd see first thing in the morning. Without explaining the situation to him, I told him to go into the field next to his house and look for five yellow flowers by themselves. That if he saw them, to take a picture and send it to me. Upon going to bed, Nikki and I both said a prayer together and thanked God for our experiences.

The next morning I woke up to a text from Chris. I opened the message, and sure enough, there was a picture of five small, daisy-like, yellow flowers in the field. I couldn't believe it, and I showed Nikki, we were both blown away. I thought I still had the picture and scoured my files looking for it but couldn't find it. I even asked Chris if he still had it, and he couldn't find it either, so unfortunately, this is one of those things you'll have to take my word on, but it happened. The one thing I can show you is the picture I drew of the vision in the field that night.

The First Appearance   By Josh Louis

The original now hangs in my bedroom, titled "The First Appearance" and is a favorite of mine.

Over the next couple of days, I noticed a change in how I felt. I accepted the idea I would receive the same intuitive gift that Nikki had, but the idea of this "purge" was something I wasn't as open to. I didn't give it much thought, but I found myself starting to let small things get to me. Things that normally didn't really bother me started renting space in my head. Whether it was as simple as seeing friends out somewhere and I wasn't invited or even being passed over in line getting coffee, I was taking everything so personally. It was obvious my ego was hurt in these situations. I tried ignoring it at first, denying that anything was bothering me. But I knew that wasn't making it go away.

Around this time, I had decided to create a Twelve Step meeting of my own. I called it Life Anonymous, and it was to be a program/meeting for anyone and everyone. The basis of the program was, we followed the Twelve Steps but not for alcohol or drugs. It would be for people who understood they were powerless over People, Places, and Things, and this was broad enough that no one was excluded. The only requirement to attend was to have a desire to improve the quality of one's life. Regular, non-addicted people that had watched others improve their lives through the Twelve Steps could now attend meetings of their own and not feel alienated. I had secured a small log cabin next to a church to meet regularly twice a week and began working on our unofficial Big Book in preparation. Something else I started doing was writing in a journal. Because I wanted to log all of my experiences in starting this new meeting, I figured journaling would be helpful. I tried keeping it to just Life Anonymous, but what I was feeling with this purge started to bleed into my writing.

When I first started to put all of this information together, preparing to write this book, I had a hard time recalling some of the emotions I felt during this strange period in my life. So I turned to that journal to reference some of the entries from that time.

> 1-20-14: *These past few days have been somewhat difficult for me. I've been going through a purge of some kind. A purge of the ego, I've been told…*

> 1-30-14: *My prayers and meditations are sporadic, and I find it hard to believe some of the things I hear from Nikki and Connie. I have felt a wide range of*

emotions like jealousy, shame, separation, anger, and fear. I really can't remember a time in recent years where I've ever felt this way.

About fifteen days in, I would ask Nikki to check with Jesus and see when this thing would end. I was told in a loving way that I was still resistant. That it was me still being defiant and that I was prolonging it. Even though I wanted to contest this and call bullshit, I felt it was true, and it got me even more frustrated.

2-5-14: Well, it's two days from the theatrical opening of my film, and I'm excited. Still dealing with this undercurrent of fear, anger, and self-centeredness. I can't help but feel betrayed in a way, like I've been forsaken somehow. I'm also angry I still haven't figured out what it is I'm not getting—ready for whatever this is to be over.

At this point, I was ready to throw in the towel—no more channeling or talk of it. I was angry and didn't really know what for. I couldn't stand talking about it anymore with my friends and spiritual advisors. Eventually, I just said I'm done. Meaning, I accepted whatever was going to happen. Once I did this, I felt a wave of peace wash over me.

2-18-14: I really don't know where I'm at with everything, but I definitely feel better. I found that once I accepted some basic truths I had forgotten about surrendering, the fact I'm not really in control, I was able to truly let go. I still don't know if I've learned what it is I needed to, and I still have my doubts regarding all of this stuff, but I believe everything is right where it's supposed to be at this very moment.

Once I truly felt acceptance in my heart and let go of trying to control the situation by having to figure it all out, something finally happened. Here is the entry that reminded me of how it all unfolded.

> 3-11-14: *Well, it's happened. As crazy as it sounds, I've received a gift, an ability. Connie and Nikki have been given the gift to channel celestial beings, and now I've been granted this ability as well. It's incredible, the last two days, I've been practicing, and I'm getting better. My doubt keeps popping up, but I just keep praying for the strength to push through. I thank Him for such a gift.*

For me receiving this ability wasn't a burning bush experience. I didn't experience the same dramatic effect Nikki did when she received hers. I remember having a conversation with Connie, and she felt a message come to her that this purge had finally come to an end. That I was ready to begin receiving messages and to practice with Nikki. Intuitively, I felt the purge was over, and something had shifted as well. It's hard to explain, but I just had an inner knowing.

Later that night, after having that conversation, I tried connecting with a deceased family member of Nikki's. I don't remember the details, but I do remember the few things I got were correct. But I knew it would only be a matter of time before Nikki would run out of deceased relatives for me to call on. I needed to find a way to learn more about developing this ability but had no idea where to begin. Even though I still had a healthy amount of skepticism, I knew something extraordinary was happening, and I needed to treat it as such. Personally, I believe we all have this ability of intuition, but it is our job to seek and develop it. The person I was led to next would confirm that very notion.

I decided to go online and start looking for ways to learn how to improve. I saw there were classes offered in person but only in limited areas, with some courses offered online ranging in price. I asked God to direct me where I should go and quickly found a psychic medium offering readings for a modest price. I wasn't looking to get a reading, but I kept poking around on her page, not really knowing what I was looking for. Then suddenly, I found it.

This woman was a graduate of the International School of Clairvoyance, which was run by a woman named Debra Katz[16]. I clicked on the link and was brought to a website detailing the different courses she offered. On the page, the phrase "you are psychic" was there with additional information explaining how every person has an intuitive, psychic ability they were born with that could be developed. In addition to offering group classes once a week, she also had private one-on-one lessons. The private lessons were what I opted for, and it was only a matter of days before I was signed up and scheduled to begin.

Now at this point, I wasn't exactly ready to perform psychic readings on anyone, nor was I hearing God's rumbling voice in my head yet. I knew the few intuitive things I had received thus far were correct but were also just brief blips of thought. To me, it didn't feel like there was anything too different from regular thoughts and psychic visions. When Nikki asked me if I had tried speaking to Jesus yet, I was now the one who wasn't ready and didn't like being pushed. *Oh, how the tables had turned on me*, I thought.

In fact, many other things I judged Nikki and Connie on I was now experiencing myself. I remember saying to them, "if I had this ability, I would just trust it" or "if I had this ability, I

---

[16] To learn more about Debra Katz, see chapter *Influential People*, page 182.

would use it all the time." Well, what I found out quickly was, the reason they doubted themselves sometimes was because of how the information came in, veiled in our own thoughts. I also found out that as much as one is excited about the prospect of doing any kind of intuitive work, one's energy will not sustain it unless there is a regular meditation practice. I prayed every day, sometimes multiple times a day but never had I practiced a true form of meditation. The reason I hadn't asked for Jesus just yet was the fear that he wouldn't answer me. After all of this, that fear almost didn't seem justified, but it was there nonetheless.

ANOTHER LEVEL OF COMMUNICATION

The time came for my first lesson with Debra, and I was ready. The phone was fully charged, my headset was plugged in, my favorite chair, this was going to be a four-hour call, and nothing could be more exciting to me. I, of course, offered Nikki the opportunity to participate in the classes, but like Connie, she seemed to have this natural ability she was happy with. She wasn't as interested in learning someone else's techniques as she was in developing her own. I respected that, but I was eager to learn more, and I knew the only way for me to do that was to learn from somebody who understood intuition.

When Debra and I got on the phone, she had such a kind and warm demeanor. Very conducive to learning, and we immediately clicked. She began prepping me to do a reading on a name she was going to give me. This was going to be a situation where she gave me just the first name of someone, and I don't know if they're dead or alive. A cold reading, I was told.

The way it was explained to me, there's psychic energy that we can pick up on, information that is out there everywhere in the universe. Any correct information that suddenly comes to someone that didn't previously know it, basically intuition. Then there's mediumship where someone can connect and communicate with individual spirits. As I mentioned earlier in the book, there are different intuitive senses a person might have. There is clairvoyance, which is seeing, clairaudience, which is hearing, clairsentience, which is feeling, and claircognizance, which is knowing. There are others but those are the main ones. She went on to explain these to me in more detail, and then told me to close my eyes and prepare to ground myself.

This was all new to me, and even though there were moments I wondered if what we were doing really made a difference, I knew I wouldn't learn unless I remained teachable. So even if this stuff sounded kooky to me, on some level, I needed to believe. She had me start out by sitting straight up in my chair with my feet on the floor. With my eyes closed, she brought me through a guided meditation where I was told to extend a chord from my body into the ground. From there, I was directed to run energy up from the earth and down from the heavens into my body. I remember feeling a sensation all over, like when you get goosebumps or the chills. But this felt a bit different. It felt like energy was actually coursing through my body.

When we finished grounding and running energy, she had me envision being inside my own head, right behind the forehead. Installed in my forehead was a window that I was able to walk up to and see out. There wasn't much that I saw, just a desert with mesas. This window represented my third eye. The third eye, known as the pineal gland, is believed to be where the soul enters and leaves the body. Whether it's the bindi, the small dot the Hindus put on their foreheads marking it, or a bible verse referencing it,[17] most cultures know the great significance of this part of the body. Once I was brought to this place, she had me now envision a white flower. There, outside of the window, stood this flower as I focused on this particular vision. She then gave me the name Manny to focus on, nothing else.

Once she said the name, I saw the letters go directly into the flower. All of a sudden, I started seeing quick flashes of pictures. I got a glimpse of a sombrero and a teenager playing guitar. I saw him riding a four-wheeler through the desert and then somewhere else smoking a joint. When I looked at the boy closer, I could see he was around sixteen, maybe seventeen, and was of mixed nationality. For thirty minutes straight, I cold read the name Manny, and at the end, she told me who he was. He was her son. He was alive and well still living in her home. I instantly felt bad about ratting on him smoking weed.

All I did was focus my attention on the images I was receiving and relayed the information back to Debra. The whole time I was getting this information, it felt random, it felt off, and I didn't know if I was getting anything of value. Debra proceeded to go through each of those details and confirmed they were all correct. She told me they themselves lived in a very rural desert area of California. That her son Manny rides his four-wheeler all the time throughout their property. That hanging on his wall in his room was a large sombrero where he sits on his bed and plays his guitar all the time. She didn't know if he'd been smoking pot but wasn't too worried about it, that he was seventeen, almost of legal age, and was a very good kid. Lastly, she mentioned that Manny's father was from the Philippines.

---

[17] Matthew 6:22 KJV - The light of the body is the eye: if therefore thine eye be single, thy whole body shall be full of light.

I couldn't believe it; literally everything I had told her pertained to her son. But how? How was I able to tell her all of this by just being given a name? Intuition. I wish I could tell you that I never doubted my ability again after that amazing experience, but that just wasn't the case. Because of how subtly the information comes in and how one has to trust what they initially get, there's a big margin for error, and that bothered me. My thought was, okay, so I was able to basically guess the right information, but how about the next time, and then after that? At what point does someone say they've arrived and are a professional? This was basically my ego, trying to control my psychic ability. My ego was saying if this has any way to make us look crazy or stupid, it's not real. It didn't want to stay in the here and now and focus on what we got right. My ego wanted to plan out the future and figure out the kinks to ultimately make me look the best at being a psychic medium. Even though I came to this understanding early on, that feeling didn't just dissipate for me.

Regardless, I was determined to work through that fear. After that initial class, I decided to just try and ask for Jesus. If I didn't get anything, I would try and not judge it. I had heard what I believed to be Christ speak through Connie and then Nikki. I felt like I knew what that energy felt like, but would I know it was Him if He spoke directly to me? Well, there I sat in a chair in my backyard. It was late one evening, and as I frequently kept looking up into the starry night sky, I said a prayer. I then just asked if He was there. As quickly as I asked, I heard a voice internally say, "Yes, Josh, I'm here. I'm always here." The voice was calm, soft, and even though it didn't sound too distinct, I knew it wasn't mine. To me, it seemed like the voice had been there all along but yet felt like a new experience, if that makes any sense. I asked, "How do I know it's really you?"

"It is I, Jesus Christ, who gave you this gift. It is My voice you will hear. I am with you, Josh."

Just like the psychic information, it was subtle but, in that moment, unmistakable. That didn't stop "logic and reason" from getting in the way of trying to discount the experience. I thought, *What if this was just my own voice somehow speaking to me?* Oh my God, what if I'm schizophrenic? But as quickly as I thought these things, His voice comforted me.

"You don't have to analyze it even though you will. I have been guiding you all along and will continue to do so." These words brought instant peace and comfort, whether it was Jesus Himself or not. At that moment, I instantly felt closer to Christ, and that was something I didn't have to analyze.

One might think a person in that position would want to ask as many questions as possible. Quiz the Son of God on anything and everything, right? Well, I didn't. I had asked every question I could think of when He was coming through Connie. I asked about the pyramids, aliens, multi-verses, where exactly we came from, you name it. I asked and got answers. I picked up where I left off when Nikki got her ability, asking her even more questions. Night after night, asking about the past experiences I had in life, the mysteries of the universe, and so on. I received yet again more answers to my inquiries.

By the time He was coming through me, there was this quiet satisfaction. I didn't feel the need to ask any more questions. I didn't need to analyze it tirelessly as I had in the past. I was content with what I was given and somehow felt more a part of the universe than I had ever felt in my life. I felt I had a place in it. I felt loved, and immediately I wanted to show that love to everyone, even the people I thought I didn't like. I just felt so plugged in and a part of everything. It was like everything I had ever been searching for in life failed in comparison to what I felt at that moment.

I continued to work with Debra on a weekly basis, teaching me more and more about my ability all the while feeling Christ's constant presence. I was taught about astral projection and remote viewing in addition to doing different types of readings and healing work. I learned about "thought-forms," which is an object you can create with your mind that exists on a higher vibrational level in the astral realm. She and I connected so well that sometimes she would give me a reading, and I'd give her one in return. She trusted my ability and knew that she could extract more detailed information from me when guiding me. When she did this, it took concentration and focus on my part and wasn't easy, but it showed me my true potential.

That would end up being and still is my ultimate challenge in doing this: focus and belief. I needed to believe I could do this, not worrying about being wrong at times. I also had to strengthen my ability to be able to focus longer. For a kid growing up with ADD, focusing wasn't always easy. But after many classes and practice readings with her, I saw how accurate I was each time, and that helped build confidence. Even with my deeply rooted skepticism at times, it was undeniable what I was doing.

Nikki was happy for me that I was advancing with my intuitive training, and I was, of course, happy she was coming into her own understanding of hers. She was doing readings for friends and family with scary accuracy. We both still sat together in the garage most nights doing sessions with the spirit box as we took turns connecting to spirits, trying to help when we could. We started taking residential cases helping people with their paranormal disturbances, and these proved to be great training for both of us. We encountered all kinds of situations, from negative entities to trapped souls. We kicked out the negative ones by calling on Jesus and the angels and helped cross spirits over by praying and focusing on the Light. The evidence we captured using our abilities and the equipment was validation that the spirits were appreciative, just like when we were with Connie. You'd think after time, we'd become immune to the shock factor in capturing this evidence, but for me, it was just as exciting with each case.[18]

But as we took on more cases, gathering more evidence and experience, I was doing more readings for people. That meant I was talking more to Jesus through my own ability. What I found was each time I gave a reading, I picked up psychic information about the person through my intuitive senses. But when Jesus wanted to share a message with someone He felt they needed to hear something, He would gently cut in. I would repeat it to the person, not knowing what it even meant, but once they heard it, it meant everything in the world to them. There were times I didn't even want to relay the message out of fear the person wouldn't want to hear it. But I knew when this happened, there was always a reason, and it was normally to let the person know, in a unique way, they were loved by an Intelligent Creator.

It was like I witnessed firsthand this great Power work through me to remind these souls they were loved. Whether the soul had a body or not, this loving Power I knew as Christ would transmit unconditional love, and in that moment, the person couldn't deny what they felt. It was remarkable, and I can't take any credit for it. I was just grateful I was somehow a part of it. It didn't matter what people asked; there was always a helpful message.

One example I remember well, I was giving a reading to a woman who wanted to speak to Jesus about different aspects of her life. One of them was "love and relationships." She explained how she had done extensive work on "being okay" with not having

---

[18] Watch our first Documentary "White Light Assistance"along with a residential case and News clip at HOPEparanormal.com/video Videos #6, 7 & 8.

found the right person yet. She shared that she was okay with it happening whenever it did but asked when maybe she would meet that person. I have been told before in readings when something will potentially happen for someone, and it has come to fruition many times. This time the answer I received for the woman was strange, and I hesitated to tell her. She noticed my puzzled look and asked what it was I got. I told her He suggested she take a piece of paper, fold it four times and then open it back up. There will be eight sections on the paper that she should write eight qualities she'd want in a significant other. Then to fold it back up and stick it in a small box and leave it there. To me, this sounded gimmicky, hokey, and pointless. I wondered if I was receiving the message clearly 'cause this made no sense. She was just as confused and asked how long she should leave the paper in the box. I was told that each section of the paper represented one month and to take the paper out in eight months. Immediately her head dropped with disappointment.

When I asked her why she was so upset, she lifted her head and, with a smirk, said, "That means it will be at least another eight months before I possibly meet someone." She told me that whether that was true or not, once it was said, she instantly felt disappointment, which revealed she really wasn't in this great place of acceptance she thought she was in. To her, that was a big deal, not deceiving herself from the truth.

By Jesus suggesting this somewhat meaningless task of folding a piece of paper, He was able to expose her own denial in a loving, un-intrusive way. He wasn't going to say, "You're lying to Me," which would've triggered a defensive position in her even if He was right. He allowed her to do it in a way that was undeniable, just like when He revealed to Connie that night at the mausoleum she wouldn't be going to Alaska just yet. The meaning behind the folded paper was so very personal that something like that to anyone else would mean nothing to them. But because she needed to hear it at that moment, it was said in such a way that it was like I was witnessing an intimate conversation between the most loving Father and one of His children. Plain and simple.

Once she understood the point of the paper, or how meaningless it was as it mainly served as the vehicle to deliver the lesson, she jokingly asked if there was anything He could tell her about the person she'll eventually meet. Surprisingly, I started seeing a man with longer hair, glasses, a few tattoos on his arms and felt he was quiet, kind, and intelligent. I will have you know, some months later, she informed me that she had met someone through mutual friends who fit this description to a T and that it seemed promising. From what I know, they are still together.

There are many experiences like this. Some I've written down so I wouldn't forget, and others are just lost. But when someone receives a message of validation, it can be life-changing. Another reading I gave made such an impact on a woman that it made her a believer in God. Prior to receiving the reading, she admitted she didn't believe in any kind of Higher Power. But what was told to her through my intuitive channeling was so powerful and meaningful to her that she believed in God for the first time in her life. She said there was no way I could tell her the things I did without the existence of a God. If you asked me what she was told that meant so much I wouldn't be able to remember. To be honest, she may not fully remember what was said either, but it was the feeling it invoked in her that she'll never forget. It awakened her inner Divinity.

I remember early on, I would just intuitively check to see if Jesus was there. His responses came quick and would normally be, "I'm here, I'm always here." We would then have a light-hearted talk or an in-depth conversation. But one day, I asked Him, "Why do you always say you're 'always here' every time I ask if you're here?"

He said, "Because maybe one day you'll finally believe Me." His response was quick but powerful, and He was right. No matter how many times I heard Him speak, captured an amazing piece of evidence, my mind still always tried to find a way to explain it away.

One day, asking to see if He was there, like a little boy checking on His father from another room, I received another powerful response. He said, "You don't have to keep checking; you know I'm here. I'm always here. To the point that others see Me with you and the ones that don't, just know it. I'm in your eyes, your heart, and your soul." I was blown away by this answer. When I heard it spoken to me, it had a real authority yet was full of love. It brought on one of the most secure feelings I had ever felt in life.

A good friend of mine, someone who was once the head of Institutional Sales for Goldman Sachs, told me a story once. He said when he came into a 12 -step program, he was a cocky agnostic who would need real proof of the existence of God in order to believe. Well, one day, after discussing the wreckage of his drinking with his sponsor, it was suggested he go to the beach and sit there and try praying. My friend, who was willing enough to take the suggestion, did just that and sat on the sand for almost an hour praying without feeling anything. As he stood up to brush off his pants, he took one last look at the ocean, and then as he was about to leave, he heard a voice. It told him to go home and begin making everything right with his wife and children. That he would also need to forgive himself. The voice then told him he was loved.

Now, to anyone else that may not seem like a big deal and certainly not a reason to say God spoke to him. But what stood out to me about my friend's story is not the words he heard, but what he thought afterward. He told me that he knew something was different about the way that message was spoken to him. That what was said was something he would never have said to himself. The reason that struck such a chord with me was, this is how I felt each time I heard Jesus speak to me.

Paramahansa Yogananda,[19] someone who will become a very important teacher for me later on in my journey, once wrote,

> *"God is perceived with the sight of the soul. Every soul in its native state is omniscient, beholding God or Truth directly through intuition. Pure reason and pure feeling are both intuitive; but when reason is circumscribed by the intellectuality of the sense-bound mind, and feeling devolves into egoistic emotion, these instrumentalities of the soul produce distorted perceptions."* [20]

What he's saying is, we can use logic and reason, but when it gets to the point we can't take in any new information for fear it challenges our beliefs, our ego is too attached, and we aren't able to see reality clearly. The understanding that there is Something greater than us out there, and not just out there but inside of us as well, is just too much for many to grasp.

What's even harder to fathom, is the idea of that Power being able to communicate with us. Yogananda goes on to say,

---

[19] Paramahansa Yogananda was an Indian monk, yogi and guru who introduced millions to the teachings of meditation and Kriya Yoga through his organization Self-Realization Fellowship.
[20] From *The Yoga of Jesus*, page 81.

"Ordinary man's occluded vision cognizes the gross shells of matter but is blind to the all-pervading Spirit. By the perfect blending of pure discrimination and pure feeling, the penetrating eye of all-revealing intuition is opened, and the devotee gains true perception of God as present in one's soul and omnipresent in all beings – the Divine Indweller whose nature is a harmonic blend of infinite wisdom and infinite love."[21]

I mentioned at the beginning of this book that when I found something to be factually based on the findings of my research, I would state it. Well, up to this point, we had collected numerous audio recordings along with visual images of phenomena proving the existence of some other dimension. We had many verifiable instances with intuitive practitioners, including myself, proving intuition, the instant knowing of previously unknown information, was, in fact, real. What I wasn't able to prove was that Connie, Nikki, or myself had really spoken to the actual Jesus the Christ.

What I found was, every time I asked Jesus for help, which meant praying to Him directly and only Him for guidance and direction that internally, I was always given it. Every time I heard that inner voice speak to me, I felt loved and connected to a Source. If we wholeheartedly ask the God of our understanding for help, what are we saying if every time He answers us in some way, we question if it's really Him? What hope is there for us? I understand what discernment is, but why would the Administrator of this Universe create such a complex system for the user if He wanted us to stay in contact with Him?

There's an old story I heard long ago, I don't remember where I heard it, but it goes something like this. A man was in his home

---

[21] From *The Yoga of Jesus*, page 82.

when a great flood began rushing in and around his house, forcing him to the roof. The man prayed to God to send a miracle and save him from the raging waters. As the water level started to rise, someone in a small boat came along and yelled to the man to "jump in" so he could be saved. But the man simply yelled, "It's okay, I have faith God will save me." The boat left, and the man continued to wait as the water kept rising. This time a helicopter flew overhead, dropping down a ladder. One of the crew members yelled down to the man, "Climb up, and I will lift you to safety." But the man just yelled back, "It's okay, I have faith God will save me." It wasn't shortly after when the water level rose again causing the man to drown. Once he got to heaven, he had a chance to talk to God and said, "God, what happened? I asked for help, and I had faith, but you let me drown." God said, "My son, I sent you a boat. I sent you a helicopter. What more did you want Me to do?"

I've always said it's simple; it's just not easy. The truth is, if we ask, we will receive, and if we seek, we will find. I know from personal experience, we have to be open to receive it or we'll miss the signs completely. I have so much more to share with you regarding what I've found through scientific and spiritual research, but I knew I had to share my story first. No matter how fantastic some of these claims were, I felt it was important to disclose them here. I wavered at times on how much I should share regarding my experiences with Christ, thinking it might be too much for some to handle. But I came to the realization that it doesn't matter.

Not long ago, a subscriber on my channel asked me if I could talk to Jesus, and this is what I wrote back to him: "I speak to Jesus daily, and when I trust and listen, He speaks back to me. He's always so loving and un-intrusive. I'm sure He could tell me what to do, but instead, He tells me He's right there and that He's not going anywhere. Sometimes, because I'm in this physical body and the illusion of this world is thick, I don't believe His words. But He doesn't seem to care. He just keeps on loving me. I said to Him in prayer one night, 'Regardless of what I do, sinner or saint, I am Thy child,' and He said to me, 'Yes, you are, don't ever forget it. I never will!'"

To me, that sums up my relationship with Him. It's between Him and me, and it doesn't intrude on my free will or anyone else's. My Creator is a loving one that knows I exist and is very involved in my life. I may have been selected on some level to experience these things, but I certainly don't believe I'm any more special than the next person. I believe we were all meant to have spiritual experiences in our life whether that be with God, Jesus, Buddha, Krishna, Mother Divine, Allah, or the great Creation Energy of the universe. Don't let severe skepticism, religious dogma, or any other prejudice keep you from discovering that great loving Power on your own.

At this point in my life, I believed I had experienced quite a bit. I even felt I had witnessed more than most when it came to the paranormal. What I didn't realize was, there was so much more I was going to be shown about my psychic ability, spirit communication, and the afterlife.

AFTERLIFE RESEARCH

I'm no expert but what I use is effective.

THERE ARE SO MANY SELF-PROCLAIMED "experts" in the paranormal and afterlife research fields that I've had to ask myself what makes someone an expert? In most other research fields, getting a Ph.D., joining a lab, spending years researching, gathering evidence, forming conclusions, and having a peer review done with the findings published is what truly qualifies someone as an expert. But there really is no such thing in the paranormal and ITC (Instrumental Trans Communication) fields. There is no accredited ghost school one can attend. There is a branch of psychology known as parapsychology defined as the investigation of psychic phenomena, telepathy, and the like, but someone would still need a Ph.D. I don't know about you, but I didn't have the grades to go that route.

Even though I'm no expert, I am someone who has spent countless hours conducting different sessions and experiments in controlled and uncontrolled environments. I've made many mistakes but learned from those mistakes, and the amount of time I've spent in the field, gathering evidence with repeatable results makes me somewhat qualified to comment on this subject matter. The fact that many of my sessions have produced true validations for people regarding their deceased loved ones makes what I do very real. I get real results, and that makes me effective at what I do. But what keeps mainstream science from accepting my findings is that even though I have to be objective with my research, I also need to use a good amount of intuition, which is very unscientific.

By going on investigations with other people, talking to members of other groups along with psychics and mediums all over the country, I found that people like to stick to what they know. True ghost hunters may ask psychics to come along on investigations, but ghost hunters always tend to be more skeptical and trust the gear and gadgets they use more. They're also more inclined to think something evil is present, I've found. With a psychic or medium, they normally trust their ability and steer clear of using any kind of equipment. Most times, psychics and mediums also state up front that they don't deal with dark entities. So, where's the happy middle?

Being able to intuitively connect to a spirit in order to communicate with them through a device is very important, and I will delve into that topic even more in the next chapter. Using a device that can give a spirit a voice without using our intuition isn't as effective, I found. But using such a device and utilizing one's psychic ability truly completes the experience, and in my opinion, the two need to be married. It's not easy though, and I understand why more people don't do it.

I had to experiment at first and see what would work for me. In the beginning, it was just a simple voice recorder and hacked radio that skips through stations. But then it led to using more advanced boxes and techniques. With that had to come the development of my psychic ability that allowed me to capture better evidence. When you say that to a true person of science, they don't accept it. But to capture great evidence, one has to be able to tap into that unseen energy. A wise man used to tell me, "The best piece of paranormal equipment we need to utilize is ourselves."

I've always said when someone tries to discount a software application or a box I use, I tell them, if I'm able to ask questions repeatedly and receive intelligent and relevant responses, then it's working. Therefore, I will experiment with unconventional methods that draw controversy from typical paranormal researchers. People that were using basic spirit boxes like the PSB7 early on thought the spirits used specific words from the radio broadcast to answer our questions. They also thought the more white noise or static the box had, the better the replies. But my research, along with Steve Huff's, has proven the opposite. In fact, the static hurts our chances of capturing better responses, and we discovered it wasn't the actual words they were using from the radio broadcast.

We found the spirits were taking the random bits and pieces of the broadcast and manipulating the audio to form their own responses. We knew this to be true when they would reply with specific words like our names when asked. The chances of my name coming up on any of those stations at that moment were damn near impossible. Not to mention the box runs with a scan rate of 150 milliseconds, so any true response will pan across three or four different stations. Meaning it's impossible for the same word, like my name, to be coming from four different radio stations at once. Another great example of how these responses were not false positives was when profanity would come through. We knew that cursing wouldn't be allowed on any radio stations and wouldn't be coming through.

THE HISTORY OF INSTRUMENTAL TRANS-COMMUNICATION

Just to give you a very brief understanding of the history of ITC, people like Nikola Tesla, Thomas Edison, Friedrich Jürgensen Konstantin Raudive, and many others were a big part of this type of research. Thomas Edison once said, *"I spent a period of time*

deliberating on a machine or an apparatus which could be operated by
personalities who have crossed over to a different area of existence, or
into a different sphere. I believe that, if we are to make true progress
in psychical research, we will have to do it in a scientific manner with
scientific equipment."[22]

Konstantin Raudive, who was a brilliant Latvian scientist and writer, studied EVP (electronic voice phenomenon) and other ways of communicating with the deceased through devices as well. He once said, *"Trans-communication is no hobby for people who cannot cope with reality, but a matter of interest and importance."*[23]

Since the time those men were involved in their research, communication with spirits through different devices has gotten better. Over the years of learning more, testing new equipment, and trying new techniques, I've been able to find what truly works, or at least what works for me. Some of the different pieces of equipment I use, as I've already mentioned, are spirit boxes, voice recorders, and night-vision cameras. I've tried so many different pieces of equipment, and for what I do, I only need a couple of items.

Normally my sessions run about twenty to thirty minutes, and throughout that time, I will have used 2-3 different pieces of equipment. I find spirits that want to communicate are normally there, and ready to talk. I have been on those "overnight" investigations, locked in a dark building for hours, and let me tell you, that's more for the person, not the spirit. You don't need to sit in an abandoned hospital overnight to communicate with spirits. For me, being at a location for a couple of hours and trying a couple of different twenty-minute sessions are ideal. It takes energy from both parties to effectively communicate, meaning

---

[22] From ITCvoices.org - first page.
[23] From ITCvoices.org - first page.

the spirit and the person need to both put energy in to get results. That energy doesn't last long during intense sessions and will need replenishing at some point. I find I don't use as much energy when I just intuitively connect and receive messages within my head as opposed to running the boxes but hearing those responses coming through makes it well worth it.

THE EQUIPMENT

The first device I'll tell you about is a box called the portal. This is pretty much a mini guitar amp speaker with a noise-canceling pedal along with a reverb pedal. The amp provides more power as the other two pedals distort the sound going through the speaker. I will connect either a scanning radio or software program to provide the raw audio for the spirit to use. If the raw audio doesn't get distorted enough, you will hear the actual radio broadcast bleed through, which can cause false positives, and we don't want that. So it's important to make sure the pedals distort the sound just enough, or the original audio needs distorting before it goes through the speaker. Regardless, reverb (echo) is needed.

Remember, spirits can manipulate any audio to form their responses. So even a recording of my voice repeating my name over and over again could serve as a somewhat effective audio recording to pipe through the box. If any word other than Josh came out of the box, then a spirit was using it. The portal has evolved over the years and is the invention of Steve Huff. Many today use a portal by making some variation of their own as Steve was so kind as to share the schematics publicly. Many of these people bashed Steve and said he was fake yet made their own portals and failed to give him credit. It is through the portal that I've received some of my most powerful evidence. It's the device I center the session around. With the amp and two other pedals, it truly allows for longer, clearer replies to come through.[24]

In addition to the portal spirit box, I use a little hand-held radio that scans stations at a fast rate called the Panabox. This is not an official name or piece of ghost equipment. It is a little cheap radio made in the 1990s by Panasonic to be used as a regular AM/FM radio. A man named John Mallory in Canada found a way to hack the cheap device allowing them to scan stations quickly like the PSB-7 spirit box I first described earlier in the book. But I think it's important before going on any further to explain where the idea for the spirit box originally came from.

As I've already mentioned, certain people in the past have worked on different devices to speak to the dead. I've given you quotes from both Edison and Raudive, but how about Nikola Tesla? He created something dubbed by others as the Tesla Spirit Radio, which consisted of a spiraled copper coil sticking out of a glass cup. There's a lot more to it, but somehow, it was picking up voices. Here is one of Tesla's quotes regarding such work, *"My first observations positively terrified me as there was present in them something mysterious, not to say supernatural, and I was alone in my laboratory at night."*[25]

In 1980 a man named William O'Neil built an electronic device called the Spiricom. He claimed he could hold a full conversation with spirits and even provided the design schematics to have his device built and tested by scientists. Unfortunately, no one was able to replicate the same results. A friend of O'Neil's later said he believed it was because William was very psychic, and his ability completed the device. If I was someone who didn't

---

[24] Watch a short video where I test the first portal I received from Steve Huff at HOPEparanormal.com/video Video #9.
[25] Nikola Tesla, 1901 article "Talking With The Planets."

know much about this work and heard that, I'd say then the device didn't work. Who knows what this William guy did to get those results or if they're even real. But now that I've done this research myself and found that I need to use my intuition to be effective, I see how that could be the case. Yet other intuitive people should've been able to use it as well. Just the same when Steve Huff creates a new device, not only does it work well for me, it works for others as well.

In 2002, a man named Frank Sumption created the first real Radio Spirit Box. I remember in 2013, I reached out to Mr. Sumption, and being the recluse he was, I didn't hear back from him right away. Frank made his boxes only when he felt inspired to and wouldn't really sell them. If he liked someone, he would gift one to them, and each box was built differently as they were created from old radios. I personally didn't need a box from him as I was able to obtain one from a bidder on eBay for a reasonable price. I purchased the 78th box he built, and it was encased in an old Air Force radio.

Eventually, he got back to me, and being kind of an ornery fellow, he gruffly asked what I wanted. I asked him about possibly taking a look at number #78 for me and making sure everything was in working order. I, of course, had no problem paying him and offered him a decent amount, but he said that he would look at it for me for free. But he stated that these boxes were ultimately created to speak to aliens, not spirits. I chuckled and told him that whether that was the case or not, these boxes communicated very well with spirits. Shortly after that call and arranging for me to send him my box, he posted something peculiar on Facebook. Paraphrasing the post, it went something like this, "They have contacted me and told me they would be picking me up in less than a week." That was pretty much it. About a week later, Frank Sumption died of a heart attack. I still have #78 on my shelf to this day. On the front, burned into it, is a little alien that he put as his little symbol.

In addition to the Portal and radio spirit boxes, I also use a voice recorder to record EVP. Spirits can use both their energy and the energy of the person to leave a voice signature on the device. Some devices are better for this than others, but it really does depend on the energy and intention of the person using the recorder. Some recorders are expensive and record very clear sound. Some are built cheaper and have a little bit of internal noise, a quiet hiss that's produced by the device. I have found cheaper devices to work better.

One recorder, in particular, is made by Panasonic, and it's called the RR DR-60. This again was a cheaply made voice recorder produced in the 1990s and was discontinued not long after being launched. The complaint was people were hearing voices that weren't their own. When Panasonic couldn't explain why this was happening, they ruled it a faulty chip that somehow mimicked human speech. Sure, that sounds about right. I have now recorded hundreds of semi-clear, pertinent, relevant answers to my questions or independent statements on their own with the DR60. These are undeniable responses that prove it wasn't a faulty chip creating these voices. Instead, it was the device's internal noise that gave spirits just enough sound mixed with their energy to manipulate and form their own words. I've even gone to different lengths to have some of my original recordings verified by audio experts.[26]

The last piece of equipment I will share with you is very important; it provides the ability to capture visual evidence—the night-vision camera. I have used different pieces of equipment

---

[26] Watch the video where I send my voice recorder to a Forensic Audio Expert at HOPEparanormal.com/video Video #10.

to catch glimpses of the astral realm, and by using simple and inexpensive cameras, I have captured some amazing things. The two best cameras I've used so far are a $250 baby monitor and a $30 home camera from Google. What I've captured with these cameras over the years are some of the brightest light anomalies I've ever seen recorded. When I say light anomalies, I'm being objective by saying they are occurrences that deviate from the standard. I know these to be orbs and apparitions.

Some people use a cell phone camera in their room with the flash on and record what they think are orbs, but in fact, they are just dust most times. But when the conditions are right, the proper camera is used, and we are open to the occurrence, we can record spheres of light.[27] What are they, you might ask? Well, many people have spent countless hours recording these orbs with digital photography, and they're convinced they're beings.

When I've captured apparitions, they were of faces of people that had passed. They appeared in a similar manner as the orbs did, as light that appears and disappears in moments. But with the orbs, there are different sizes and levels of brightness. Some move very fast, and others very slow with very deliberate movements. A few other things I've noticed regarding these balls of light: when they are present, the activity through the box is increased, and I see them interacting with the gear. When I call on someone like an angel, guide, or even guru, the ball of light captured is usually brighter than the others. Many of them have entered and exited me or the equipment during the sessions. So, whether these orbs are balls of energy, transport spheres for spirits to travel in, or actual souls themselves, they are very much involved in what I do. In another chapter, I will go more into more depth on what I've captured regarding this visual phenomenon.

---

[27] See chapter *Visual Signs and Evidence*, page 162

As time goes on I suspect there will be better equipment and programs that will enable us to speak to the other side easier. But until then, this is what I use, and it continues to work well for me. It's not perfect, and there's a whole process that goes into properly conducting these sessions and getting results, which I will explain in the next chapter. But I will express this essential fact one more time. It is our intuitive connection that allows us to capture above-average results. Without it, doing this work is difficult and can be why some try and fail to capture very much at all. I take what I do very seriously, and I remember someone once saying, "When you capture a piece of paranormal evidence, it's an honor, and it means you've been allowed to sit at the adult table." I took that to heart.

THE FOUR STAGES OF CONDUCTING SESSIONS

What I do before, during, and after spirit sessions.

SOME PEOPLE MAY THINK CONDUCTING a spirit-box session is as easy as flipping the box on and asking questions. Unfortunately, it isn't. When done right, it's a real process from start to finish.

1. PRAYER, MEDITATION & INTENT

Anyone can do this work. Should everyone do this work? Not at all. I will go into this in another chapter, but when people ask me what they should do to get started in ITC or spirit communication, I tell them to talk to God first before any spirit. For me, that's how it's always been, so prayer and meditation are a big part of my day already. I say formal prayers before my hour-long meditation, and throughout the day, I speak to Jesus, reaffirming my faith. Simple affirmations like "I trust you, Father" and "Father, let me be a channel of Thy peace" are strong and instantly bring me back into a higher vibration. There are so many distractions in this physical world, and it's easy to get off track, especially when doing this kind of subtle spiritual work. Between outside noises, kids, spouses, pets, phone calls, and technical difficulties, just to name a few, a person's thoughts can also be very distracting.

To help combat the distracting thoughts and deepen my connection to God-Source, I practice meditation. At first, I learned TM (Transcendental Meditation)[28], which took some practice but was fairly simple. We were to sit upright, repeat a mantra in our minds, and distracting thoughts slipped away. I've had many great meditations practicing TM, but years later, I discovered Kriya yoga. Kriya being a bit more involved and requiring more discipline, the transition was challenging at times for me. But I think that's just because I still like to do things my way. My meditation practice is done every morning whether there's a session or not and is the foundation of my spiritual practice. Regardless of who you are, what you do, or what you believe in, find a simple meditation practice. Even if you're an atheist, meditation is just as important as sleeping, and so many people, like myself, were never taught anything about it. The Dalai Lama once said,

"If every 8 year old in the world is taught meditation, we will eliminate violence from the world within one generation." I would strongly agree with that statement.

Once my intention is set on doing a session, I will say out loud who I will be trying to reach. I do this just so my spirit guides know my intentions. I might even write the name on a little dry erase board I keep near my desk I've dubbed the "spirit board." Do I honestly need to do this? Maybe not, but I do it anyway. It helps make my intentions clear even though I've done sessions for people within an hour's notice and in different locations.

On the day of the reading or session, I try to be as serene as I can. Shortly before the session, I will again sit down and do one more meditation, which is the quick grounding meditation that Debra taught me during my intuitive training courses. This exercise is a very powerful tool to run and balance energy. It is not

---

[28] Transcendental Meditation (TM) is a specific form of silent, mantra meditation, Maharishi Mahesh Yogi created and introduced the TM technique and TM movement in India in the mid-1950s.

something to take the place of a complete meditation practice but powerful nonetheless and can be done at any moment. All of these mindsets, prayers, and meditation practices help prepare me to do what I do. But I will say this, no matter what is going on or how I feel that day, with some days being better than others, I always go into a session with as much faith as possible. I have to trust that even though I may have technical issues with the gear or get frustrated when missing responses from the box, I will capture and hear all that I'm supposed to. This helps me let go of control, and I'm reminded I'm just a humble servant of the Divine Creator.

2. TECHNOLOGY AND EQUIPMENT PREPARATION

One of the biggest issues when conducting spirit sessions is the "technology" aspect of it. I've already shared what I use as equipment, but that had to evolve from me trying different devices. I've used so many different pieces of equipment over the years, and I suspect I'll use a lot more. But with the few pieces of gear, I utilize now, I try to make sure everything is set up properly so that nothing malfunctions during the session. Nothing sucks more than having a good connection with a soul on the other side, and the camera shuts off, or the battery on the box dies. It's very frustrating.

So hours before my session, I make sure all SD cards are cleared of all old footage, all camera batteries are charged and the computer equipment updated. I will even go as far as to make sure I know how I'm going to set up my equipment. Basically, I want nothing to distract me during the session. Even doing a brief test run for a minute or two beforehand is helpful. The key for me has been to just roll with any unforeseeable glitch and be communicative with the spirits I'm working with.

When it comes to what I set up and use, I try and use two cameras and two or three different spirit devices. This way, I have options and backups. Some spirits love to use specific devices such as the Portal and radio spirit box, and others only prefer the voice recorder. If for some reason one of the cameras goes down, there's a second camera running, ensuring there's always coverage. I've had my one and only camera shut off during a session with no sound or warning as amazing responses were coming through the box. The feeling afterward when I realize it didn't record is one of sickness—so being prepared with whatever technology I'm using allows me to be more focused on the intuitive aspect of the session, which is just so important.

3. CONDUCTING THE SESSION

I have found punctuality in life matters, even in the afterlife. Time may not be the same on the other side, which we really don't know, but when spirits are interacting with me on this plane, time matters somehow. There have been numerous occasions where I've had a private or group session scheduled and at the last moment had to push it back fifteen or thirty minutes. Some of the first responses I get in the session are about me being late, sometimes resulting in the spirit leaving. So setting times are helpful and they need to be upheld and honored.

Once I sit down to begin, I may ring a chime three times, signifying I'm beginning. The three times for me represents God, the un-manifested energy that's everywhere, the manifested which was Jesus Christ, and then the Christ Consciousness within all of us. There have been times I have forgotten to ring it, and the guides will remind me. Closing my eyes, I then do a brief grounding meditation where I picture energy from earth entering my body from my feet and then Cosmic Light from above entering my body through the top of my head. All I have to do is try and visualize it happening the best I can and have faith it's working. From there, I say a prayer out loud to Jesus for protection, understanding, and guidance and also ask Archangel Michael and my spirit guides to assist in whatever way they can. Finally, I ask for the person I'll be trying to reach.

It is important I'm not just asking for them but that I'm actually trying to connect with them psychically. For me, I have to go within and visualize myself walking across a glass plank in space to a floating astral room. The better I can focus and truly see this vision, the better my connection is. Once I get to the door and feel the brass knob, I turn it, the door opens, and I enter. I normally see two or three of my guides standing there next to a table with a Portal spirit box. On the opposite side of the room is another door that leads to all of the Astral Realm. I ask for the person I'm looking for to appear at the door, and sometimes it's right away, sometimes it takes a few moments. There have been those rare occasions where the person did not show up at all.

Once I see the person, I will usually get a few physical attributes about them. I might see hair color, facial features, articles of clothing, and they might even say something to me. I always welcome them and invite them to sit at the table in the astral room. I briefly explain who I am and what I do and tell them that my guides will help them use the equipment. I tell them to please have patience that I will try and hear them in real-time, but if I don't, it's most likely still working. So many times, while reviewing sessions in the past, I've heard the spirits clearly say, "It's not working."

From what I understand, it's about waves and timing. Waves of raw sound going through the box are being manipulated to form a different sound wave before leaving the box and reaching me. So like catching a wave when you were a little kid on your bodyboard at the beach, timing was everything. If you jumped too soon or waited too long, you'd miss the wave. Same with the box and is the reason we hear partial statements and them speaking to each other. The spirit has to get the timing right, amongst other things. Some people on the other side can use it amazingly and right away, some not so much. It seems the younger people, the ones that pass with a lot of energy, can work it well. The people that died in their later years prefer to use the simple voice recorder over the more complicated pieces.

As I call out details of the person as I notice them, the guides will confirm or deny if I'm right by sending a simple but clear response through the box. This has been one of the greatest aspects of doing this work. To be able to see something intuitively and have it confirmed audibly through the equipment is astounding. At first, my questions seem basic and vague, but it's just to establish a clear communication line, even if I don't understand every answer in real-time. I will continue through the session, still intuitively checking in with the person, but it's important I maintain operating the equipment. I've always said I can't walk and chew gum at the same time so finding a balance between the intuitive and technical aspects is always a challenge but one I manage.

After I've spent about thirty minutes running through each device, the energy is normally down a bit, and it's time for me to stop. Could I go longer? Yes, and I do so when I need to. I have just found thirty minutes is an ideal length of time for a session, plus all of the footage will need to be thoroughly reviewed. This takes a lot of time and can't just be done once or twice.

When ending the session, I thank everyone for helping, I thank the person for coming, and I tell them if I hear anything that requires me to ask for them again that I will. I say my closing prayers, including one for the person I just spoke to and the guides that helped. I ring my chime three times again and then stop the cameras. The session is done.

4. REVIEW PRACTICES & PRESENTING EVIDENCE

Now, this is the last stage of the process, and I'd argue it's the most important but all of them are. It would be pointless for me to cut corners in any area of this work, and if there was one part that really requires patience and thoroughness it's this part. Too many people have tried taking a stab at doing this kind of research but failed to present any kind of clear, definitive evidence. It's not because they didn't capture any but more because they didn't know how to find it.

One of the things I like to do right after conducting a session is nothing. In the past, I used to load all the footage up into the computer and start the review process that night, sometimes staying up for hours. But what I found was, I was usually exhausted and still emotionally invested in the session. That meant there were certain moments while conducting the session where I felt something or thought I heard something, and having those moments fresh in my mind could jade my review process. It was important when doing these reviews that I was as objective as possible. I understand that may not always be easy because I'm the one that did the session in the first place, but this is why I take so long to review everything.

I think it's important I say this before I explain my process any further. I don't hail my captions as 100% accurate. I don't claim that every response I've tagged is fact. I spend a lot of time objectively listening to responses, and when I feel I'm hearing the same thing each time I listen, then I will caption it. But these captions are my best-educated guess based on thousands of hours of experience.

When it's time to begin the review process of a session, I start by watching the night vision footage first. I do this to check for any light anomalies, and when I do this, I make sure to mute the sound. I want to only focus on the visual aspect, and turning the sound off helps me stay focused. When I find an anomaly, I just put a quick marker there and move on. Sometimes I find the most amazing orbs move around me or into the spirit box. It's always a gift to capture something that special.

When it's time to review the audio aspect of the session, I like to listen with external speakers first. Headphones are a big part of the review process, but certain responses sound different through different speakers, so it's important to use both. I will first listen to the session, tagging any obvious responses and using question marks for anything I feel is a possible response but can't make it out just yet. I don't slow anything down yet either. This first pass usually takes about two to three times the length of the session as I have to go back over responses multiple times and re-listen. I share with others who do this work that if you can't make it out the first two or three times listening to it, leave it alone for a bit. Your mind will start trying to form a word or phrase from it.

Psychoacoustics is the study of how humans perceive sound. Because we have spent thousands of years evolving having to survive, our instincts are to look for faces and listen for speech. This is where pareidolia comes into play. Seeing faces and hearing voices when nothing is really there. It is essential that anyone who does this work capturing audio and visual evidence is aware of these potential pitfalls. When starting out, it's easy to make these mistakes, and a lot of people do. But over time, one becomes more discriminatory towards the type of evidence they accept as actual evidence.

After my first review, I won't listen again until the next day. This time I will use my sound engineer headphones, and this will be the review when I slow responses down if need be. It's time-consuming and tedious, but when I hear an amazing, clear, direct response to a question I asked, it makes it all worth the while. With each undeniable and intelligent response, it proves there's another dimension from which beings can communicate.

It's important when reviewing audio files not to do so over a period of two hours. Any audio expert will tell you this. Sound truly starts to get distorted at that point. It is important for me always to have fresh ears when reviewing sessions. During this second review, I will listen without reading my previously placed captions. After I feel I've heard it correctly, I'll then see what I previously tagged. If it matches up, that is good. If not, I change it back to question marks as it may just end up being a partial response or not even a response at all. After this second review, I have a better understanding of what came through and will have been able to fill in some of those other question marks I tagged in the first review. But I'm still far from finished. A session isn't thoroughly reviewed until I've listened to it several times for weeks. It's also essential I listen and do this work during the day when I'm fully awake. I might still scrub through a session at night, but I don't trust my ears when I'm tired, so I leave all the heavy lifting for during the day. It's very important to do all I can to get these captions right if the spirits on the other side are doing all they can to get the messages through.

Once I feel the captions are as accurate as I can possibly get them, I look to trim any dead air from the video. Dead air would constitute moments where no one is speaking or if I asked a question and didn't get a response. For research purposes, footage is never erased. When trying to have the findings of one's research validated, any cut in the footage could mean possible tampering. But the majority of my sessions are for clients and my followers. So instead of an uncut video that is forty minutes long, I condense it to twenty minutes and only include the results. When I've worked with audio experts in the past, I've sent the raw footage of me conducting experiments with the recorder itself. I've also done some live sessions showing just how all of this works through demonstrations, and I'm sure I'll do many more in the future. But the reality is most people have short attention spans, and when I present what I found in a short, clear-cut manner, it's always received better.

One of the things I suggest for clients to do when watching their session is to have a pen and pad handy to write down the responses. That way, the person can go back and read it like a transcription, which really helps digest what was said.

This process only came about through trial and error, lots of error. But I learned because I was willing and dedicated. I know sound experts that have told me you can go to school, but the best education is real-life experience doing it, and that's what I've certainly done. It's a shame because there are so many people within the last ten years who have really gotten into ITC and the paranormal fields but don't take the time to review their sessions properly. Not only are they missing key responses spirits expended lots of energy to leave, but they're showing poorly tagged sessions that make this work look invalid. My inner voice would say, "Ease up, Josh. They're just starting out or don't know what they're doing yet," but many do and still don't take the time. The reason is that it's tedious and a lot of work.

To me, a properly run session that is thoroughly reviewed and then presented in a powerfully clear-cut manner is a great service to humanity. It's not easy conducting successful sessions, but when it happens, not only do both communicator and spirit benefit, but thousands upon millions of people that get to see the work for years to come do as well. I know that sounds like a grandiose statement, but it's the truth. These sessions have helped me continue to spiritually evolve, not to mention spirits on the other side saying thank you. But that's almost nothing compared to thousands of people who have sent messages and left comments telling me what these sessions have done for them and how life-changing they were. For that, I am very grateful.

HARD TO BELIEVE
IN THIS

How logic and ego work and the walls
that need to come down.

UNLESS YOU COME FROM A free-spirited family
with a spiritual background or had an actual psychic medium
in your family, chances are you were told from a young age that
ghosts don't exist. Especially when we were kids, and we thought
we saw something in our rooms at night. Our parents would tell
us it wasn't real, so we'd go back to bed. When we were told ghost
stories, they were to scare us with evil characters. So right there,
in our formidable years, we were being shaped to believe spirits
were fake unless it was evil, then it was real. I'd say those are two
major walls right there.

As we get older, we begin to make our own decisions about
what we choose to believe. One example of something that might
happen, we see a video someone sent us or a picture someone
shared of a ghostly figure or even a UFO. We can't believe our eyes,
and this seems like undeniable proof of their existence. We think
maybe our parents were wrong all along. We share it with others,
trying to raise awareness of such a discovery until an uncle or a
friend shows us proof the video was faked or the picture altered.
When we do our own research and find out they were probably
right, we vow never to be taken for a fool like that again. To us, all
evidence is now fake and can't be trusted. It's not worth it.

Another example could be, we may have a paranormal
experience ourselves. We are sure of what we experienced, whether

it was something we heard, saw, or felt. Afterward, we share our experience with trusted confidants like friends and family. But these are some of the same people who told us this kind of stuff wasn't real, or evil. What we tell them falls on deaf ears or is written off as being impossible, causing us to question our sanity. We then start trying to find an explanation for what happened and find it's easier to believe it was really nothing. The last thing we want to feel is crazy or have others perceive us as being crazy. This is normal but really nothing more than our egos trying to protect us.

In addition to those obstacles, there are knowledgeable individuals out there who have used their degree of intelligence as a pompous weapon to try and devalue any intuitive, spiritual, or paranormal experience one might have. To be naturally a skeptic and want to find a simpler explanation is actually quite healthy, but these individuals have already made up their minds that this stuff is not real. What I have found is despite the fact they are very intelligent, they lack open-mindedness and humility—two essential qualities when finding out the truths of our very existence. As mentioned earlier in the book from an excerpt on how people can be too smart for their own good, knowledge alone cannot save us.[29] Whether we as a society or as individuals want to admit it or not, intuition plays a large part in our lives.

Instead of giving you examples of how we're held back from exploring our intuitive nature, I'll give you examples of how our intuitive nature works even when we don't realize it. But first, I'll explain a little of what I've come to understand through my research and the other sources I've found on how intuition works.

Basically, all forms of life are made up of atoms. These atoms have electrons that orbit a nucleus. When one atom's electrons say to

---

[29] See excerpt from Yogananda on page 91, middle paragraph.

another atom's electrons, "Let's vibrate at the same frequency," they use a messenger particle made of light called a photon. These photons that are constantly entering and leaving our bodies communicate with every single atomic particle around us. We don't see this process because, in addition to not seeing microscopic particles, we only see a very small fraction of the full electromagnetic spectrum. What we can see we call visible light, and even in that light, which looks white to us, a spectrum of seven separate colors exists as seen in a rainbow. The other waves unseen by the naked eye are known as radio, infrared, ultraviolet, x-ray, and gamma. That means we're only seeing and processing a minimal amount of the information riding on the full light spectrum.

When they say we're all connected, it is in my opinion, along with many others, that the fabric connecting everything is the Flower of Life. Also known as the Life Flower, it is a Sacred Geometrical pattern made up of spheres. This is the fundamental geometry of space-time and would explain why this important design was strategically placed in decorative art and architecture by many different ancient civilizations. What I'm saying is, all of the empty space around us isn't really empty at all. It is filled with a fabric, a network of spheres that bind us all together, which brings me back to the subject of photons.

As these bio-photons leave our bodies, these light particles carry our intentions with them through the network. Everyone reading this book, I'm sure, can attest to these examples I will now give you. We've all felt when someone walks into a room, and can pick up on their energy, whether negative or positive. Someone might even say that guy gave off a weird vibe (vibration). This is the intuition working without the conscious part of us knowing it. Or how about this example. We've all experienced thinking of someone right before receiving a phone call or text from them. Or vice versa, where someone tells you they just thought of you right before you called them. These are hard examples to deny being that most of us have experienced them, yet there are those analytical types I mentioned earlier that would just write these off as ordinary coincidences.

The reason this phenomenon happens is that we are all connected by a field in which different particle waves travel. The second we intend to call someone, the intention is out there, and with action behind it, it becomes more powerful. This is why they tell us to be careful what we think, that we don't want to (project) negative thinking into the Universe. In the light particles leaving our bodies, our intentions travel along the network of space-time and reach the person before their phone even rings. With the person that walks into a room giving off a certain vibration (vibe), it means their light particles traveled along the network and interacted with everybody's energy field. When a legitimate psychic medium picks up on detailed information about an event or deceased person, they are using the fabric/network of space-time, and light is always involved.

Reading and learning about all of this stuff over the years and then being able to validate it through my research has been one of the most rewarding experiences of my life. If any of this seems too difficult to believe, I'd urge you to research quantum entanglement. In quantum physics, entangled particles remain connected so that actions performed on one affect the other, even when separated by great distances. This means science has effectively proven an electron can exist in two places at once. This phenomenon was so mind-blowing Albert Einstein called it

"spooky action at a distance."

So, with all of this knowledge, the undeniable examples of intuition working in our lives, and all the documented cases that have captured mind-blowing evidence all over the world, why is all of this still so hard to believe? Well, as I stated, the walls that were put up early on in our lives and the fear of looking crazy to our friends and family play a big part. But as long as mainstream science continues to ignore credible findings in afterlife research, the masses will continue to ignore the fact consciousness does indeed continue after our bodies die.

There are many obstacles one must get past to find the ultimate reality in life. The ancient rishis (seers) of India called the reality we live in Maya (cosmic delusion) because there is a thick veil masking our true identity, which is Spirit. The more we live in our five senses (touch, sight, hearing, smell, and taste), the harder it is to use the sixth, which is intuition. This is why practicing some form of meditation is key, as it takes us within and away from the five senses. Meditation truly helps us to connect with our true nature, regardless of what one's spiritual or religious beliefs are.

Going one step further, I'll say that even though I've had crazy spiritual experiences, captured remarkable evidence, and given thousands of powerful readings with detailed facts, I still have a hard time believing in this stuff myself sometimes. I believe in the core findings of my research, and I believe a Power greater than myself is working in my life, but I still have periods of doubt. By sharing that with you, I'm letting you know that Maya, the illusion of this world is thick, and I need constant reminders of my Divine origins. Some people are naturally faithful and don't require recordings, videos, and psychic phenomena to believe in an afterlife. But for some, believing isn't possible until they have an experience of their own, and even then, it may not be enough to leave a lasting impression.

Early on in my life, there may have been certain beliefs instilled in me regarding God, religion, and what happens to us after death, but it was my own research that provided the most reliable information. I didn't want to rely on someone else's version of God or interpretation of what they thought the afterlife was like. Instead, I chose to go to the Source myself, literally. This meant having faith in something bigger than me but still willing to ask tough questions that challenged core beliefs. Even though I still have my moments of doubt, I know I'm supposed to share them with the people that follow my work. While experiencing these uncomfortable moments, it is possible to still have faith and carry on. One of the affirmation prayers I'll say sometimes is "Lord, I believe, help me with my non-belief," and I find I'm always given the reassurances I need. [30]

So, in order to believe in the unseen, we need faith. Once we exercise that faith, we have to then seek answers and keep earnestly doing so. If we truly want them, it is imperative we begin to listen to our intuition. When we do that, we start to receive real responses, and even though it still may be hard to believe, it will become impossible to deny the greater reality we discover.

---

[30] Watch a very informative video where I address questions from skeptics at HOPEparanormal.com/video Video #11.

FACT VS. BELIEF

"What we call basic truths are simply the ones we discover after all the others."

Albert Camus

SO, I HAVE SPENT YEARS researching the paranormal and ITC fields, gathering evidence. I have formed conclusions based on that evidence and on my channel and this book is where I've reported my findings. I have also had the pleasure of having my evidence reviewed by my peers and reviewing theirs. I know this doesn't make me an expert, but what it does make me is someone qualified enough to state the facts uncovered from doing this research.

We are intuitive people who can send and receive information telepathically. There's no question or doubt about it. I understand there are fakes out there, as I said, I devote a whole chapter to it, but the reality is psychics and mediums exist. I'm one of them. On countless occasions, I have perceived information that was detailed in nature and impossible for me to know. It wasn't a fluke or a good guess. What was said was not only correct but very meaningful to the person. I have also had psychics give me information about myself no one knew. I have countless documented experiences that prove we are intuitive people who can receive information we previously didn't know. In addition to that fact, I will also include that with proper training we can effectively move items without touching them. This is known as *telekinesis*. I will discuss that in another chapter as well.

We are able to effectively hear and record intelligent voices from an unknown dimension or space. Whether people want to think these voices are spirits, aliens, or demons, we can record them. These are not just random responses from the radio, computer application, or sound pareidolia. Not everything that comes through the spirit boxes and voice recorders is spirit, but as I've stated earlier, when I ask a question and receive an intelligent, clear, pertinent response, it's communication. This has happened thousands of times now for me to the point I've had full-on conversations. It's undeniable. Bottom-line.

Consciousness exists after the body dies. This is being proven by science now, and I'm sure in years to come, it won't be as contested as it is today. But for the sake of only commenting on my own research, not only have I received correct information from deceased people intuitively, but I've received countless validating responses through the spirit communication devices. Information that only the deceased people would know proving some part of them exists somewhere after death.

Not everything that comes through is evil. This is a huge misconception perpetuated by religious people, misinterpreted bible verses, and ignorance of the inner workings of this communication. Out of all the years of doing readings and spirit box sessions, only 10% of it has maybe been negative. When I say negative, I don't mean growling and attacking, but more like a negative comment a person might make on social media. Yes, I've experienced some dark entities, and they've made the session interesting, but most of that 10% has just been a negative person like any negative person we may encounter in real life. The majority of the communication has been positive, with messages of Light from deceased loved ones or helpful messages from spirit guides. There is also no question that this spirit communication and intuitive work has made me a much better and more spiritual being.

These "voices" speak of angels, Jesus, and even God. Forget all of my personal experiences with what I've perceived to be God; there is plenty of real audible evidence of a Higher Power. Not only have I heard numerous times over the years angels being mentioned through the boxes and recorders, but God and Jesus have also been mentioned quite a bit as well. Some ask for God or even Jesus, with others saying they've seen God or met Jesus. For me and so many others, we are taught about God from some religious denomination. If we are blessed enough, we might even have a personal experience with that Higher Power. But to capture audibly clear, undeniable responses referring to that Power as being real, well, in my opinion, that is compelling evidence for the existence of some God. The reality is those voices all could be lying, but they've been talking about it since I started doing this work. Many of the "voices" have said they've seen Jesus next to me at times. My belief is they aren't lying but just sticking to the facts; these "voices" speak of Divine Beings and a Creator.

There are Light anomalies that interact with me during sessions. I have now captured numerous orb-like lights on digital photography and video, and I'm not the only one. Many others have captured the same phenomena, and these lights are not dust, water droplets, or some kind of insect. From when I first started capturing them using an expensive full-spectrum camera during residential investigations to doing sessions inside my own home using cheap night-vision cameras, these orbs have served as undeniable visual evidence of something paranormal. Whether they are souls or just some kind of vehicle for astral entities, I can't say for sure. I have my theories, but I will discuss them in another chapter. For now, the facts are these lights have ranged in brightness, size, speed, and have interacted with my body and equipment hundreds of times. I suspect they will continue to.

I personally believe my research and work in these fields prove a lot more than these six facts, but if someone asked me quickly to tell them definitively what I've learned beyond a shadow of a doubt, it would be this. I have discussed quite a bit in this book already and will continue to do so, but these six undeniable truths I've shared here are a part of our reality whether people want to admit it or not.

FAKES & FRAUDS

My experience with the charlatans in this arena.

IT'S A SAD AND ANGERING truth, but the reality is there are many who fake evidence out there for a multitude of reasons. Fakes and charlatans have been around since the great spiritualist movement began in the late 1700s. These so-called mystics would con people out of their money, citing certain spells while others faked spirit photography using translucent cheesecloth. It's nothing new.

When I opened up my hookah bar, there was a woman who rented the small space next to me. In her window hung a neon sign that flashed "Psychic." I saw people coming and going throughout the week until one day, an angry customer of hers returned. Suddenly her door wasn't open for business, and when I talked to the irate lady, she explained how this "psychic" told her she had a curse placed on her. That the only way to get rid of it was to give the psychic a thousand dollars to hold on to for a month. She went on saying that when the month was up, she tried to get her money back, but the psychic told her she burned it due to the money being cursed as well. *Yeah, I'm sure she burned it real good at a department store.*

When it comes to videos being shared online, they normally have to do with evil hauntings, demon attacks, and so-called "possessions." Most of the stuff being shown is dramatized and fabricated, in my opinion, but that's what some say about my work, so who am I to judge? What I will tell you is that there were many videos online that I've watched hoping to see something real, and instead, I saw evidence being faked, and badly at that.

Listen, I'll be the first to tell you, coming from a filmmaker, getting views and creating entertaining content is just part of the deal when it comes to running a channel or building an audience on social media. But never have I had to stoop to faking evidence for views. If I ended up doing videos like the ones I just spoke of, my channel would have triple the amount of subscribers. But it's just not an option. I'm sure some people started out legitimately researching the afterlife, and while posting videos, they saw the most views they received were when they showed a nasty EVP from a spirit. From there, the wheels start turning in their heads, and they feel they need to supplement the evidence to make it interesting. What they don't realize is they're no longer doing anything authentic and have desecrated something very sacred in my opinion.

I'm going to share a crazy story with you, something that happened at a time when I was just starting to understand more about my psychic ability. But first, I will share a powerful experience, one that preceded this crazy story. I was friends with an older couple named Jane and Jimmie. They were sort of like my spiritual grandparents. Jane was constantly smiling and brought wonderful energy with her always. Jimmie, being a true southerner, was incredibly charming and possessed tons of experience he loved to share with people. When I started the Twelve Step meetings focused on emotional recovery, Jane and Jimmie were always there to help and support me. One day at the meeting, I noticed Jimmie was looking thinner than usual, and I mentioned it to him. The following week he went to a doctor to get checked and was told he had less than a month to live. Cancer. Within a week, he had deteriorated so quickly he was barely able to speak, lying in a hospital bed.

When I got the call from Jane that he wanted to see me, I, of course, rushed over to the hospital immediately. Jimmie knew very well what it was I did regarding afterlife research and psychic development and always found it fascinating. At one point, he wanted to talk to me more about it, but we never got the chance. I wondered if that was the reason he wanted to see me. When I got there, family members were gathered around the bed, and Jane quickly asked everyone to step out of the room so we could spend a few moments together. As I searched for the right words, I instantly felt none were needed. I sat on the bed with him, held his hand as he laid there. He looked over at me and I at him, and he gently nodded a couple of times. The message was understood. He then just rested his eyes. It was a beautiful moment I will always cherish.

It wasn't more than an hour later that Jane called me calm but emotional letting me know Jimmie had passed. She shared with me that at the time of his passing, she placed her hand on top of his head. Just as he let out his last breath, she felt his energy flow out of him. Over the years, Jimmie had touched many lives, and there were over 500 people at his funeral. He was a special man.

Weeks later, I was heading to bed, and as I got in, I felt someone to my right side. Intuitively I heard a voice say, "Hey, Josh, it's me, Jimmie." I even saw him as he looked like he was back to his regular self. I couldn't believe it and asked if it was really him. He said yes and told me he needed me to tell Jane something very important. I told him, of course I would, and then he blurted out, "Tell her she's being ridiculous." I asked what that meant, and he said, "She'll know, just tell her." He then thanked me, told me he loved me, and was gone.

The next morning I called Jane and told her what happened. I then relayed the message verbatim. "Jane, you're being ridiculous." She sighed and began to cry while laughing at the same time. I was dying to know what this message meant, and she told me that within the last week, she hadn't felt him around her. She started thinking maybe he had left her already. His reply to her, "you're being ridiculous," meant he hadn't gone anywhere. It was so important to him to get that message to her he was able to effectively come to me and communicate with me. What an honor it was to be able to relay such an important message.

Months later, Jane was still feeling the pangs of grief from her loss. They had been married for fifty years, and it was a strong connection. We've all heard the stories of a married couple being together a long time; one passes, and within days or even hours, the other passes as well. With Jane still in so much pain, she sought out another medium to try and bring Jimmie through for another message. A friend of hers recommended seeing this young reverend at a spiritualist church who was also a medium and gave readings. He didn't charge but did accept a certain amount as a donation towards the church. After going to see him, she raved at how amazing he was, how accurate he had been, and that I had to go see him.

The following week I called the church and booked an appointment with the Reverend George.[31] After driving some time, I arrived at what seemed to be an older house on a large piece of property. Inside, someone greeted me and gave me a brief tour of the building where I saw an altar and pews just like a traditional church would have. The person was very nice and asked if I was there to get a reading, to which I replied yes. Leading me to a waiting area, he handed me a small piece of paper, a pencil, and an envelope for my donation. I asked what the paper was for, and he told me to write down three people I wanted to try and reach along with a question. Once I had done that, he advised me to fold it three times and hold on to it as I went in to see the Reverend.

---

[31] For legal purposes, Reverend George is not his real name.

That sounded strange, but like a kid watching a magician perform his act, I'd be looking for any funny business.

On my paper, I wrote Adam, Jimmie, and Jesus with one general question for all of them, "Was there an open message they wanted to give me?" I folded it three times and was then walked back to the Reverend George's office, where I was greeted by a young man with a kind smile who was dressed well. On the wall hung a picture of Jesus. I sat at the Reverend's desk across from him holding my paper. He introduced himself, and then politely asked for the donation envelope. Once I gave it to him, he then asked if he could touch the paper with the names on it. A bit wary of the request, I gave it to him as he held it above the desk. I saw it in his hand the whole time the few moments he held it and then gave it right back to me. As he seemed to focus in a similar way I did when I intuitively connected, he started to receive something. He felt I had a psychic ability as well and then looked over at the picture of Jesus on the wall. He stated he felt Jesus was with me, that I work with Him in some way. From there, he asked me how I found him, and without receiving an answer from me, he brought up Jane. Now I never stated who referred me when I called, nor did I remember giving them my full name. Before I could say anything, he blurts out Jimmie's name, letting me know he is coming through as well. The message from Jimmie was "thank you."

All of what the Reverend gave me made sense and, in some instances, was scarily accurate. The only thing was he didn't get Adam, my friend, to come through in any way. But that didn't matter; I had never seen before what this young man had done. I was impressed and inspired. Once the reading was over, I picked up my folded paper from the desk where it had sat the whole time and then left.

On the way back home, I replayed the meeting in my head, wondering how he was able to tune in so well. Not to mention he was so personable and just a real pleasure to work with. I thought one day I want to be just as effective as he is. When I got home, I called him up and asked if he would allow me to pay him for one-on-one lessons. He was reluctant at first, but I could tell he liked me and eventually agreed to teach me. He told me he held service Sunday mornings and that afterward he had an open time slot. That I should attend the service and then we could do the training in his office afterward. I called Jane and told her Reverend George would take me under his wing, so to speak, and train me to be a better psychic. She was so happy and even offered to pay for some of the classes.

Sunday came, and I arrived at the church early. I couldn't believe how many people were there attending. Upon entering the church, the same greeter met me at the door along with some other parishioners. Everyone was so nice as I was helped to an open pew and sat patiently waiting for the service to start. It wasn't long before the Reverend came out and began his sermon. I couldn't believe it. It was actually genuine sounding with humor injected throughout. The message was poignant, and everyone hung on his every word—he was that good. Towards the end of the service, he channeled open messages from people's deceased loved ones. Two different parishioners that morning received brief messages that seemed to really resonate with them.

After the service, I watched him chat with each person leaving the church and saw how many really loved him. Once most of the parishioners left, we went back to his office, where we immediately went out the back door so he could have a cigarette. It was during this conversation I saw more of a human being as opposed to some highly revered spiritual leader. We talked about our lives, what we liked and didn't, we laughed about stuff that we both related to using our abilities. It was like I found a friend, and it was someone doing things I would love to do one day. I thought the idea of the church being non-denominational but recognizing all ascended Masters, a church that supports intuitive gifts and doesn't shun them, was so needed. From what I saw, it was definitely a place I could work with and support.

In the first class, George accepted fifty dollars as the fee and taught me some wonderful techniques on focusing to connect better. I'd go once a week and did so for about five weeks. Over that time, he didn't accept another dollar from me as payment, and we continued to connect as friends. He even came into my hookah bar one night to check it out. The stuff he taught me, kind of like with Debra, my previous teacher, was accurate and seemed very helpful. The only problem, intuitively I had started to get things wrong or not even get them at all. Up until that point, when doing psychic work, I was rarely wrong with what I got. It wasn't like everything I got was always correct, but this bump in my journey was noticeable.

One of George's techniques that differed from what Debra taught me was don't sit silent when doing a reading. Debra always taught me to take my time, and if I had to sit there quietly looking internally before speaking, it was fine. George taught me even if I wasn't getting anything psychically at that moment to keep talking as it helps to keep the flow of energy going. He felt I was preventing myself from receiving information at times. When I asked him what I should be saying when I'm not getting anything, he told me anything would do. Just fill that space until something does come to you. This made no sense to me. I can't just tell people anything until I finally get something.

Each of those weeks I attended training with him, I went to service beforehand. Each service was moving, his sermon well prepared, and his open messages at the end to people in attendance always had a touching effect on them. At this point, Reverend George offered me an entry into the church as a pastor in training. Apparently, this church wasn't the only one; there were others. About ten other churches around the country were all a part of the same organization. If I did choose to follow the path he was suggesting, I would need to go to North Carolina to study for a month where the main church and seminary school were located. There I would be taught by Reverend Martin, George's mentor and head of the organization.

To me, all of this sounded interesting, and a lot of what he spoke of I wanted to do. Of course, I was still a partner to Nikki and a father to Eva and still owned businesses and had other responsibilities. But if I could embrace more of my spiritual gifts and follow a true purpose in helping people, this might be it. I had some serious thinking to do. It almost felt like when I was told I would go to Alaska with Connie and live in a community. But regardless, life's an adventure, and the way I looked at it through new lenses now, I felt I shouldn't be closed off to new experiences and opportunities.

After a class one Sunday, George told me he felt I was ready to give a sermon at Sunday's service; I couldn't believe it. I humbly accepted the honor and immediately started thinking of what my first sermon would be on. Once I gave it some real thought, it became clear I would speak about my personal experience with Christ. This also meant I would be giving the open messages at the end of the service just like George did each time.

Over the next week, I really worked hard on what I was going to say on Sunday. When the day came, I was sitting in George's office, and he could tell I was nervous. So many people were there in the pews, including Jane. It was important that I did a good job, I felt. Finally, it was time to go out there, and as we were both walking to the main room, George stopped me. He told me he saw a woman near the back whom he knew had a deceased husband named Paul. I asked him why he was telling me this, and he then said, "Well, I see you're nervous. When it's time to do the open messages if you get stuck like you have been, just go to her first, and I'm sure you'll get something."

This really bothered me, but quickly, I got over it as it was time to give my sermon. The Reverend opened it up, introduced me, and I was off and running. I'd love to tell you that I captivated every soul inside that church with my powerful words that day, but I'm afraid I looked more like a scared kid reading his book report in front of his fourth-grade class. I'm sure someone got something out of what I said that day, but when I was done, it was time to give the open messages. Still reeling from what I just went through at the podium, I couldn't get out of my own head. As George re-introduced me to begin giving messages, I started my brief process of connecting intuitively, nothing was coming to me though. I started talking as George had suggested to try and get the energy flowing, and I started sounding like I was a magician getting ready to do a trick. "Okay, well folks, today I'm going to connect to your loved ones, and once I do, information will start coming in, and if you know who it is, please speak up, blah blah blah…" Still, nothing was coming to me.

In the back stood that woman with the deceased husband named Paul. I didn't want to go to her because I felt George had fed me that information. I don't know why I was acting that way. When a client wants to connect to a loved one, I need to know the name in the beginning anyway. I just felt like George didn't believe in me in that moment and wanted to make sure I had something to keep me from failing. For me, that was always

God. I didn't need anything else. I always felt if I wasn't receiving information while doing a reading, then I wasn't meant to get it.

Regardless of why George did it, I still wasn't receiving any psychic information at that moment. I then looked at the woman and said aloud, "You have a husband that passed named Paul, correct?" She gasped and said yes. Well, that was all I had, and unless I got more, that was going to be the quickest open message ever given in that church, I'm sure. But in that moment I got a little pain in my chest and I touched it. I said, "Paul died of a heart attack, didn't he?" She confirmed he did. I then felt him tell her to start wearing her cross necklace again. I relayed the message, and she gasped again. Immediately she confirmed that she had a necklace with a cross given to her by him that she stopped wearing out of frustration with God. I was blown away and so grateful that those details came through.

Directly after getting that, I felt a boy who drowned many years ago make himself known to me. I felt it happened in a backyard pool; I even saw the initial E. When I said all of this, a woman stood up and told me her son Ethan died thirty years ago in their pool when he was just eight. He just had a message saying he loved her. All the info about her son and what I described him looking like was enough validation for her. I was so pleasantly surprised and full of gratitude I could do what I had been doing since being told of my ability.

Walking back into George's office, he grabbed me by the shoulders and said, "Great job, man. You really surprised me with that last message. I didn't know that woman had a son who drowned. I'll have to remember that." He then told me that he thought I was ready for him to show me about physical mediumship. This is where a medium allows a spirit to channel through them fully and even physically manifest with the help of the medium's energy. For it to work, though, it must be done in complete darkness, he explained. He suggested I meet him at the church on Thursday at 9 PM. I was again intrigued and agreed to meet him.

That Thursday, I remember taking that long drive to the church, thinking how amazing it would be to continue growing my intuitive ability. I honestly could say that after all I'd been through, after all the blessings I had received in my life up to that point, there was no greater gift than having the ability to communicate with my Higher Power and receive answers sometimes. I took that time in the car while driving over to pray and thank Jesus for all I was experiencing. I then prayed that He continues to lead me down the right path with all of this.

I arrived at the church this time with no one else there, just George waiting for me outside, smoking a cigarette. What I liked about the Reverend more than anything was that even though he was loved and respected in the church, he didn't pretend to be a perfect person. He was flawed like the rest of us and seemed to use that to his advantage when relating to his parishioners. Our class that night began in a room with almost no visible light. It was just the two of us sitting in chairs facing each other in the dark with an item he brought known as a trumpet.

A trumpet is an object in the shape of a cone and is usually made of aluminum. With help from the medium, this object is supposed to help spirits project their voice. This was something that was very big at the height of physical mediumship during séances. George had placed the trumpet about six to seven feet away from him, so it wasn't in arm's reach. Just sitting there, listening to each other breathe in the dark, was strange, and I couldn't help but feel awkward. But I was there to expand my ability, and sometimes that requires stepping out of one's comfort zone.

The Reverend directed me to just sit there for a few moments in silence and focus on the trumpet in the room. Eventually, a spirit will try and use it, but it requires our energy for it to work, he told me. As we sat there, I wondered, would this really work? After a few minutes of nothing happening, I heard a rattling sound but it was quick, though. I heard George in front of me breathing, but the sound came a distance away from where the trumpet was. After a moment of silence, it happened again, but this time louder and longer. This time there was no doubt it was the trumpet moving. It sounded like something was trying to pick it up and move it, but whatever it was didn't have enough strength. We sat there for a little longer, and nothing else happened. George then got up and told me to shield my eyes that he was turning on the lights. With a smile, he said, "That's enough for tonight. It's getting late."

I was still sitting in my seat and honestly didn't know what to think. I couldn't believe what just happened with the trumpet, and apparently, that was obvious to him. "So, how do you feel?" he asked. I told him that I was trying to process what just happened. I knew anything was possible, yet I wondered how something like this could happen. As I went to put the chair back up against the wall so we could leave, he stopped me and told me he wanted to talk.

We both sat back down, and the first thing he asked me was if I'd given any more thought to the seminary. I told him yes that I was interested in it, but it would be difficult as I'd have to leave my family and business responsibilities while training. He told me he understood but shared with me that he had been looking for someone, somebody like myself that would want to be a part of what he was building. He told me that even though I may not be able to attend the seminary right away, it wouldn't prevent me from participating in church services. Heck, I already had given a sermon, I thought, maybe this could work.

He went on to explain that if I wanted to start doing my own readings at the church as he did, that I could so. If I wanted to run a workshop on what I do or offer some other intuitive service to parishioners that I could so. At that moment, I just felt so blessed. George was kind enough and saw something in me that he wanted to take me under his wing like this. I thought about how great it would be to have an actual brick and mortar place I could come to, where I could continue my research and have a full house of people to share it with. As I was thinking this, he told me he wanted to talk to me about something else. I could see he was kind of nervous as he shifted in his seat a bit.

He started off by telling me how much he had come to respect me and what I do. He went on to tell me he had a good feeling about me when I first came to get a reading from him but didn't know if I was the one. The day I gave open messages after the sermon was the day he said he knew.

I was confused and asked, "The one for what?"

"The one to infuse this church with new energy, but first I needed to know if you could handle it," he replied.

Still confused and not fully grasping what he was saying, again I asked, "Handle what, being a pastor here at the church?"

He then shifted in his seat again, telling me what he was about to say was really difficult but felt that it was time. I nodded in agreement, and with him looking down, he muttered the words, "Josh, I look people up."

I remained calm as I asked for what would be the third time for George to explain his veiled statements. Only now, I was starting to get an inclination of what he was trying to tell me.

With what I just felt during that "trumpet" experience, I knew whatever it was, it wasn't a spirit.

"George, what are you trying to say? You look people up, what does that mean"? I asked calmly.

"I Google them and gather information before they come in to see me for a reading," he explained.

"What about the folded piece of paper"? I asked.

He went on to tell me that he switched the paper and quickly looked at it and switched it back before the client could suspect anything. The piece of paper is called a billet, by the way, and has been used for years by charlatans. Many people don't know this, including myself, at the time. With me, he told me it was a bit more difficult because it seemed I never took my eye off my billet. He could see what he was telling me was starting to bother me and insisted he wanted to tell me sooner but didn't know if he could trust me. The day I accepted his help with information about a woman in the crowd, he felt I belonged. Before I could set him straight and tell him he was sorely mistaken, I noticed there was more he wanted to share with me. Personally, I'm someone that wears their heart on their sleeve, always have been. But this time, I was doing everything in my power to use self-restraint, and just neutrally listen. I decided that once he was done, I would certainly express what I thought of him and his operation in full.

As we sat there in this half-lit, empty room, Reverend George shared all the dirty secrets of not just his church but all the others in the organization. He revealed a longstanding syndicate of morally and spiritually sick people. George was brought into the church by Reverend Martin, the elder that runs the head church in North Carolina. There, along with other apprentices, he was groomed to effectively pull off these acts of fraud on parishioners all over the country. George spoke of a book that each Reverend would keep with people's information in it. Information, such as details about their lives for easy reference before readings. Some of these parishioners would religiously go to these psychic spiritual leaders for weekly readings and relied heavily on the information they received.

As angry as I was at that moment, I could tell George felt safe telling me all of this. I still had questions and wanted to know more and continued to maintain my composure. I noticed with certain readings or open messages he had given, some of the details were not information found online. Personal things like what a loved one might say or a personal item no one would know about. I asked him how he knew those things. He told me he was indeed psychic. When Reverend Martin discovered him, George was a cocky young man who had an ability. As Martin encouraged George to continue to develop his intuitive ability, Martin convinced him at some point, he would hit an obstacle.

"When people are coming to you for help, encouragement, and answers, we must deliver no matter what," Reverend Martin told his young students. That meant using one's psychic ability but having an ace up the sleeve just in case the information runs dry.

This is why right before entering the room to do open messages, George asked me if I wanted any information. All he told me was the woman's name and that her husband died, which is information I would need before any normal reading but looking back on it, he probably had more information he wanted to give me. He thought by me accepting that information that I was indeed like him. Someone who had a real ability but would play ball when giving the parishioners what they wanted. George went on telling me how he didn't want to do this anymore and just wanted to help people, but without giving them these amazing readings and open messages, many wouldn't attend the services and continue to support the church. By bringing me in as a fellow pastor, he was hoping I'd bring more legitimacy to the church while I turned a blind eye to some of his magic tricks that helped support the church financially.

After all of his explaining and justifying, he then asked me what I thought about his proposition. I was internally upset, I was hurt, I was angry on all levels, and yet I stood up calmly and asked him to walk me outside. He got up, and together, we walked out the church doors. Outside, George lit a cigarette, and even though he had divulged all the inner workings of his fraudulent operation, I still had one more question.

"How did you get the trumpet to move?"

Without saying anything and a tinge of shame on his face, he went into his pocket and pulled out a collapsible pointer like one a professor might have to teach a class. He opened it and demonstrated, while in a dark room, he would lean over without anyone seeing and move the tin trumpet, which was six feet away.

I couldn't contain myself any longer, yet I wasn't going to scream and yell as I had normally done in the past. I methodically explained to the Reverend that what he was doing was immoral and absolutely deplorable. That no, I would not be joining his church nor helping him defraud people on any level. I was surprised his organization hadn't been taken down yet and told him upfront that I would out him to Jane and some of the other parishioners. He hung his head as I'm sure this wasn't the way he pictured this night going, and I started to my car. I then stopped and turned to him with the last bit of compassion I had left in me and said, "I hope you take this opportunity and change your ways. There are many that may not forgive you for what you've done, but God will." I then got in my car and left.

On the ride home, I felt lower than low. Sure I told him off and stood up for what was right, but I felt horrible. I felt like an idiot. *How could I be so stupid and fall for this carnival act?* I record real paranormal evidence, I legitimately receive verifiable information intuitively without ever having to look anything up, yet here is this charlatan conning people with sleight-of-hand tricks each week. It's no wonder people like James Randi spent their lives trying to catch these kinds of crooks. It's also no wonder I get hate slung at me on a daily basis, being called fake and despicable. That's the type of anger it brings up in people; it's certainly how I felt driving home that night.

While in the car, replaying everything over in my head, I yelled out, "JESUS, WHY HAVE ME GO THROUGH THAT?" I didn't receive an answer, and again, this time a bit quieter, I asked, "Father, why did I need to experience that? How come you didn't show me the truth sooner?"

Softly I heard Him reply, "I wasn't going to let it go any further, but you needed to make a choice." This was yet another test, and even though I don't think Jesus Himself sent me to the Reverend to get scammed, I do believe He used this already unfolding experience to teach me. Just like it says in the bible, "We know that all things work together for good,"[32] and even though I was still upset, once I heard His response, I instantly said, "Thank you, Jesus." I was already letting go of the anger surrounding the experience.

I was sure to inform Jane and those other parishioners of the Reverend's misdeeds and never set foot in the church or speak to George again. The last I heard, many stopped attending the services and getting readings, but some didn't believe the news about their trusted Reverend. The reality is there will always be fakes out there, and it's a real shame. It causes skeptics to become extreme in their disbelief and stop objectively looking for the

---

[32] Romans 8:28 KJV - We know that all things work together for good to them that love God, to them who are the called according to his purpose.

truth. It takes a grief-stricken person and turns them bitter and angry. Yet when those same skeptical, grief-stricken people find someone, who like myself, prides themselves on showing nothing but real and authentic evidence, lives are changed.

My advice to anyone searching for answers about what happens after we die, or the truth about their deceased loved ones, is to do their own research. And even though it's okay to have people such as myself aid in that search at times, never fully rely on one single person. Rely on a Power greater than yourself, such as God, to guide you, and you will always be shown the truth. It just may not be on your time. This experience with the spiritualist church really put a dent in my confidence psychically. For a period after, I felt I wasn't getting as strong of messages, but all I could do was turn that doubt over to my Higher Power. Eventually, I was brought out of it and began doing some of the strongest psychic work I've done to date. So don't let the Georges out there sour your soul's journey. Instead, let them teach you the inconvenient truths about the ego and greed. Because, honestly, no one has the right to deprive you of the truth. It's yours to seek.

PROOF IN THE BIBLE

How could the naysayers get it so wrong?

WHETHER YOU BELIEVE IN THE authenticity of the Bible or not, I think you'll find this chapter very interesting. Every day I'm pelted with comments like "what you do is evil, the bible says so," "you're only speaking to demons," or "Leviticus 19:31," which is a verse in the Old Testament that reads, *"Do not turn to ghosts or consult spirits, by which you will be defiled. I, the Lord, am your God."*

That verse and a slew of others thrown at me on a regular basis seem pretty straightforward about not doing this type of work, but when I explain a few simple facts, you may just have a different opinion on what you think the bible says about it. There's quite a bit I could say on this subject, but for the purpose of keeping this book around two hundred and fifty pages, I will only bring up the main points. The bible speaks of the afterlife, a Purgatory-type place, communication with spirits, and urging to pray for them. Of course, you make the final determination on what to believe, but when I get to the final verses, it will be pretty hard to misconstrue or misinterpret what is said.

It is important that I state though, the bible is not the only authority when it comes to holy texts. To suggest that the bible is the only book that is correct when it comes to holy matters is not only arrogant, but also ludicrous. That suggests all other ancient belief systems are wrong, which is absurd. So for the sake of being objective, which I believe to be still even though I love Christ, I will cite other ancient holy texts that are extremely powerful and resonate as truth. Not only do they resonate, but many of my scientific findings have also confirmed what each of these books states regarding God and the afterlife.

There are other amazing books that I may not list here, but please do not read into it. I'm just mentioning some of the books I've had the pleasure of studying on some level and find they hold truth: *The Bhagavad Gita*, the *Tibetan Book of the Dead*, the *Gospel of Thomas*, the *Holy Science*, the *Autobiography of a Yogi*, and the *Yoga of Jesus*. Each of these books talks of a Power greater than ourselves, a multi-leveled afterlife, and the processes by which we move through those levels. So I would suggest checking out each of these books over time, but again, right now, we are speaking about what the bible says on these matters.

Many important books (chapters) were taken out of the Bible, and it was man that did it. These writings in the Tora, the Old Testament, were believed to be handed down by God Himself like the Ten Commandments given to Moses. Whether you believe that or not, man certainly had his hand in bringing it about into print. In 70AD, Jews and Christians were using the Old Testament called the Septuagint as the New Testament hadn't been formed yet. In 90AD, the Jews went through all the books looking to take out anything Christians used to prove Jesus was the Messiah. They found seven books to take out, which included 1 and 2 Maccabees, which described Purgatory and ministering to the dead. They claimed these books were not canonical.[33]

Around 300AD, Constantine helped move the Roman Empire from paganism into Christianity. For historians, the reasons are unclear, but many believe he did it for more control over the people. It has been widely agreed that Constantine left out verses, possibly books from the bible, which he personally

---

[33] Included in the list of sacred books officially accepted as genuine by the Roman Catholic Church.

didn't agree with. Right there, we have tampering again. The Roman Catholic Church was formed sometime after, and in 1517, a man called Martin Luther tampered with it some more.

Up until that point, Purgatory was known as a place in between Heaven and Hell and was such a place to work out unresolved sin. Luther didn't like the implications and, on October 31st, made an argument that faith alone was enough to get to Heaven. While faith is of the utmost importance, we still need to put action behind it. For if this was the case, we could literally say and do whatever we wanted and know because we believed in God or, more specifically, Jesus Christ, that our faith alone would save us. Well, faith without works is dead, as it says in James 2:14-26.

But the idea of purgatory was understood amongst the Jews and Christians until Luther had all mention of it removed from the bible. All because it went against what he personally believed. That means the bible that most people use today, the King James version, is missing key pieces of information Jesus and the Apostles lived by. This version of the bible didn't fully come about until the 1600s with the belief we aren't allowed to have relationships or contact with our deceased loved ones until the mid-1700s. I'm going to get to the verses here shortly, but first, it's important I explain some of what happened leading up to where we are now regarding the contents. Now, remember, many other things happened in between some of these events I'm giving you as it would take many books to cover all of it, so I'm just giving you the main factual points.

In addition to the amendments and omissions over the centuries, there have been many different bible translations. Have you ever heard the term "lost in translation?" If I were to say to you, "I know someone who is a very sly person," what would be the first thoughts that come to mind? Possibly that the person is sneaky or deceitful, not good qualities. But if we were back in the 13th century and I said the same statement, it would mean the person I described as sly would be skillful and wise—both excellent attributes. The word is related to the Norse word "sleight" as in "sleight-of-hand," a phrase I used in the last chapter to describe the sneaky and deceitful Reverend George, who was a con man.

You can see how meanings get lost in translation. Words written in ancient Hebrew didn't always mean the same as what they meant when they were translated. Just so you know, there are different ways of interpreting the bible. First is through *Sola Scriptura*, the belief that the bible literally holds everything one must follow to live properly. This means the person can't believe anything that's not in print. There's *Sola Fides*, the Lutheran idea that our faith alone saves us regardless of our deeds or acts. And then there's the *Literal Interpretation*, the idea that one must believe everything in the bible, taking it at face value and literally. If the longest amount of computable time in the bible is 6,000 years, then that's how old the earth is (which we know is not the case).

Why am I sharing with you about the different translations and interpretations? Well, not all, but many of the verses the naysayers come at me with are from Leviticus in the bible. This was old Jewish law that didn't even apply to Jesus and the Apostles. I would say 95% of the people that throw those old verses at me don't live by that old Levitical code either. Examples, you say? Well, if they did follow the laws, they wouldn't wear make-up, use hair-dye, have earrings or tattoos, eat pork, shrimp, or lobster, couldn't shop, work, or even use electricity on the weekends. There are over four hundred of these types of laws that very few people actually obey today.

So with that said, we also understand that some of these verses were interpreted differently than what they meant at the time they were written. Why does the King James version (KJV) use the word "necromancer" instead of medium in Deuteronomy 18:10-13? Because medium, as a term for intuitively speaking with the deceased, wasn't used until the mid-1850s. Yet, the word medium to describe a necromancer shows up in many different versions that came after the KJV. A necromancer is nothing like a medium and shouldn't even be considered remotely the same. In ancient times, a necromancer was someone who forcibly conjured the dead using spells and magic to manifest spirits. There was even a belief in reanimating a corpse through sorcery. A medium is someone who gives and receives messages from the other side; that's it.

In the KJV, in Deuteronomy, which is in the Old Testament, it says, *"there shall not be found among you anyone that taketh their son or daughter pass through the fire, or that useth divination, or an observer of times, or an enchanter, or a witch, charmer, consulter with familiar spirits, a wizard, or a necromancer."*

But in the New International Version (NIV), the same verse says, *"let no one be found among you anyone who sacrifices his son or daughter in the fire, who practices divination or sorcery, interprets omens, engages in witchcraft, or casts spells, or who is a medium or spiritist or who consults the dead."*

Notice how the word medium is now in there along with spiritist. So the translator made the decision to use medium and spiritist instead of necromancer, yet those terms weren't used until much, much later. You can see how the original terms lose their original meaning with new words. Why the mention of not sacrificing your son or daughter? Because that verse was originally written at a time when people threw their children into fires as sacrifices. Something else we thankfully don't practice in modern times.

Not only would this necromancer, also known as a "ghost wife," force familiar spirits to tell her about future events through spells and magic, but at the burial site, she would try and fully re-animate the body. *Yikes.* A medium does none of the things a necromancer does. The point of a researcher is to explore and help others learn from the research. The point of a medium or intuitive having an ability is to help people communicate and receive confirmation that life does indeed continue on the other side.

Now before moving on to the New Testament (NT), I briefly want to mention one last verse in the Old Testament (OT) that reveals quite a bit about the afterlife and communication with spirit. 1 Samuel 28:8-20. This is where Saul, after outlawing necromancy and driving any practitioners out of town, is desperate for answers on a matter and disguises himself to seek a ghost wife for counsel. When he reaches her, he calls on Samuel, who is dead, and is able to communicate with him through the woman. Even though this woman's services have been outlawed by Saul, she still helps him, which shows her in a compassionate light. It also reveals a friendly and helpful intuitive exchange with the other side.

So as we get ready to look at a few strong verses in the NT, I reiterate the reason naysayers get upset when they come across a video of mine and feel compelled to leave a bible verse is that it challenges their core religious belief. The belief that just believing in Jesus will get you straight to Heaven, regardless of what you do. When they hear real evidence from spirit coming through, to them, it can't be true, or they'd be wrong in their beliefs. So it's just demons every time, they think. What the naysayers don't realize is eight of their books from the OT are missing. These books are the ones that talk about the importance of praying for the dead and a place to go after death to work through unresolved sin or emotional baggage.

Remember, when I first started looking for answers using mediums and spirit boxes, the most prominent reply I received from spirits was "help." I didn't have to do anything with that information. I could've been like one of those National Geographic camera guys and just watched the deer die of dehydration in the name of research. But, instead, I decided to do something and started praying for these spirits. I talked with them, and even though I didn't fully understand what was always said, I received enough confirmation that I could help in some way.

Some have said, "How you do you know you're not talking to demons who are looking to trick you?" This is a fair question, and the answer is in the bible in the NT. In 1 John 4:1-6 NIV, we are told to test the spirits: *"Dear friends, do not believe every spirit, but test the spirits to see whether they are from God... every spirit that acknowledges Jesus is from God... we are from God, and whoever knows God listens to us; but whoever isn't from God does not listen to us. This is how we recognize the Spirit of truth and spirit of falsehood."*

It isn't unheard of to get a negative spirit. I have dealt with them in the past, so have other researchers, but the majority of the spirits I have coming through speak of love or mention Jesus. His name is mentioned all the time. Some ask for Him, and others mention that they have seen Him. Someone once said, "But yeah, the demons can lie and still say His name," and I just had to stop her.

Listen, if you feel demons can say and do whatever they want all the time with no protection, everyone is screwed. Yes, there is free will here and in the afterlife, so someone, good or evil, can lie, but we see evidence of a great equalizer called karma or spiritual law. Everything I've ever done when it comes to this research or intuitive work has been with my Master Guide Jesus Christ. That means I call on Him, and yes, He may have others help me such as angels, guides, and other ascended Masters like Babaji and Paramahansa Yogananda, but I am a humble servant and child of the Lord's.

Which leads me to our last couple of verses and possibly the most important. These verses prove that the gifts myself and so many others have received for thousands of years are indeed of Divine origin. Paul writes in 1 Corinthians 12:4-11 NLT:

> *"There are different kinds of spiritual gifts, but the same Spirit is the source of them all. There are different kinds of service, but we serve the same Lord. God works in different ways, but it is the same God who does the work in all of us.*
> *A spiritual gift is given to each of us so we can help each other. To one person the Spirit gives the ability to give wise advice; to another, the same Spirit gives a message of special knowledge. The same Spirit gives great faith to another, and to someone else the one Spirit gives the gift of healing. He gives one person the power to perform miracles, and another the ability to prophesy. He gives someone else the ability to discern whether a message is from the Spirit of God or from another spirit. Still another person is given the ability to speak in unknown languages, while another is given the ability to interpret what is being said. It is the one and only Spirit who distributes all these gifts. He alone decides which gift each person should have."*

I mean, wow, Paul says it all right there. We are all given gifts from God that can range from wisdom, knowledge, faith, healing powers, miraculous powers, seeing the future, and discernment of spirits, which involves communicating with them. He says all of these gifts are from God, the same Spirit, and we are to use them for good.

Let's look at another telling us we should want these spiritual powers from God. Paul continues in 1 Corinthians 14:1-3 NIV:

"Follow the way of love and eagerly desire spiritual gifts, especially the gift of prophecy... everyone who prophesies speaks to men for their strengthening, encouragement, and comfort."

Here, Paul is telling us to desire intuitive abilities, that these abilities, when used to minister to people, strengthen and encourage them. I cannot tell you how many people have messaged me over the years, expressing to me their faith has been restored, or they feel more connected to God from seeing a video of mine. I can't take credit for it as I know it was God working through me, but what a beautiful example of taking someone broken (me) and turning them into a working radio for His messages. I think that's exactly what Paul was talking about in these letters. Paul himself was someone who, being consumed with the idea of money and power, had a blinding white light experience with the ascended Jesus, and his life was changed forever.

I think I've shown plenty of real, clear examples of how the bible has been changed, edited, and misinterpreted throughout the years in certain parts. I've also shown powerful examples of how God gives us various intuitive gifts to help people.

This last excerpt is not from the bible but a quote from Deacon Kristina Rake M.A., who is a bible scholar and has a Master's degree in theology. It took all my knowledge from over the years to write this chapter, but it was her book "God and the Paranormal Part 1: Mediums, Ghosts and the Afterlife in the Bible" that truly filled in many of the holes for me. I urge you to add her book to your ever-growing list.

> "If Jesus and the Apostles, as well as the first Christians, all practice prayer for the dead and believed that prayer assisted those who had died, then anyone who assists the dead reach heaven is performing a required Christian ministry."

IT'S NOT ABOUT RELIGION

Breaking down the wall religion has
put up; it's a spiritual journey.

I WILL TRY NOT TO make this chapter too long as there is quite a bit that could be said on the subject of religion. Throughout the book, I've already mentioned that even though I believe in Jesus, I also believe in Buddha, Krishna, and the other Ascended Masters. The reality is, there are spiritual laws that govern the universe, so regardless of who you are or what you believe, those laws don't change. Just like if I dropped an apple on someone who was Jewish and then on someone who was Christian, the law of gravity wouldn't change. The apple would hit both people at the same speed and force.

Now, let's look at another bad analogy of mine. Like the laws of driving on a highway, vehicles travel on a multi-lane road heading in one direction. There are different types of vehicles moving at different speeds and interchanging lanes. Some of the cars get off the exits while others are getting on. But the flow of traffic is steady, and eventually, the road will end in one location. Without taking the analogy too literally, the religions and spiritual practices we believe could be the vehicles in which we are brought along the ultimate path back to the Creator. Some of these vehicles move fast, and some meander a bit, and when stripped of the paint, leather seats, and flashy features, all the vehicles are essentially the same. Four wheels, a chassis, an engine, and a steering wheel (free will). Essentially at the core of all these religions is love and tolerance. It's man that ultimately taints that with his ego, corrupting what is pure. The fact is, unconditional love is ultimately the only energy that will bring you back to God. Being in a vehicle will definitely bring you along the path faster as some people try to get on the highway and walk it alone. I compare this to just trying to live a good life and not giving much thought to a Higher Power or spirituality in general. The pedestrian will eventually reach their destination, but people riding in the vehicles will have reached it much sooner.

That's not to say religion is the answer because unless you have the gift of discernment, to be able to judge good from bad, it may be tough to spot a fraud. Just like with Reverend George and the spiritualist church, God eventually showed me the truth about. But to actually make progress on the spiritual path, one must find a process that works for them. If one wishes to progress even faster on their journey and reach the destination quicker, one should find a Master that they feel connected with. The term Master is not because they rule over us but because they've mastered themselves.

The Buddha said, "Suffering is due to attachment." It is the ego that keeps us attached to desires. If these desires go unfulfilled before death, they will cause us to reincarnate back into a body to resolve them in our next life. These desires, along with the karma we carry, can cause us to keep coming back here. Reincarnation doesn't exist, you say? Nonsense, of course, it does. Not only do Buddhism and Hinduism, two of the oldest eastern religions, believe in reincarnation but so did Christians until most mentions of it in the bible were removed. The church didn't want people thinking they could do whatever they wanted in this life and still get a do-over—the same reason for getting rid of purgatory. But some clear verses mentioning reincarnation still remain.

In Matthew 17:12-13, the Apostles ask Jesus about Elijah, who has already been dead for a while. They want to know when he's coming back. Jesus answers, letting them know Elijah has already returned as John the Baptist and wasn't recognized. Here in Matthew 26:52 NIV, Jesus references not only reincarnation but also the deciding energy that dictates each individual life we live. Karma.

Jesus said to him, "for all who draw the sword will die by the sword."

He is not saying that if someone kills another person in this life, they too will also die in this life the same way. We all know that's not true. But just with those eleven words, Jesus tells us we live multiple lives and that every action, whether good or bad, dictates what happens to us in this life and the next. That is, until we Self-realize and overcome all attachments and preceding karma.

In Revelation 2:7 NIV, God says:

"To him that overcomes, I will give the right to eat from the tree of life, which is in the paradise of God."

He's saying anyone who overcomes the ego-self gets to ascend and be with Him. Here in Revelation 3:12 NIV, God says:

"Him who overcomes I will make a pillar in the temple of God. Never again will he leave it."

Anyone who overcomes the attachments of desire will join Him in heaven and not have to reincarnate again.

In the Bhagavad Gita V:16, Krishna says:

"In those who have banished ignorance by Self-knowledge, their wisdom, like the illuminating sun, makes manifest the Supreme Self."

Krishna tells us, by letting go of the ego (soul identifying with the body), we become illumined and manifest our true Self, which is a part of the Creator. Whatever you want to call that Energy, whether it's God, Brahma, or Yahweh, it doesn't matter. They are just names for what we can't fully comprehend. But regardless of what we call that Creative Intelligence, He created Himself into smaller light-waves of consciousness and now wants those waves of souls back with Him. But because He gave us free will, He must wait until we choose to return to Him.

In the Gospel of Thomas, we are told where we come from. In Verse 50, Jesus says, *"If they say to you, 'Where did you come from?', say to them, 'we came from the Light, the place where the Light came into being on it's own accord and established itself and became manifest through their image. 'If they say to you, 'Is it you?', say, 'We are It's children, we are the elect of the living Father.' If they ask you, 'What is the sign of your Father in you?', say to them, 'It is movement and repose.'"*

Here in verse 59, Jesus tells us to seek God now:

"Take heed of the living one while you are alive, lest you die and seek to see Him and be unable to do so."

As He refers to God as the living one again, Jesus tells us to find our Father now and not wait till after death, where it becomes more difficult due to having unresolved emotional baggage. That's when we become one of the voices asking for help through a spirit box.

The good news is that being free to follow who or whatever we want when it comes to God and religion, we don't have to figure it all out to begin seeking. The living God Jesus speaks of is not solely found in a church or with a certain clergy member. God's energy is everywhere. Listen to how Jesus speaks for His Father, in verse 77. *"It is I who is the Light which is above them all. It is I who am the all. From me did the all come forth, and unto me did the all extend. Split a piece of wood, and I am there. Lift up the stone, and you will find me there."*

Because Jesus was fully Self-realized, He was able to speak His Father's true words telling us God's energy is Light found in everything and everywhere. Here is a bible verse, 1 Corinthians 12:12, telling us God, more specifically, Jesus was not just for Jews, Christians, or Catholics but for everyone as He was a fisher of all men. *"The body is a unit, though it is made up of many parts; and though all it's parts are many, they form one body. So it is with Christ. For we were all baptized by one Spirit into one body–whether Jews or Greeks… we were all given the one Spirit to drink."*

All these verses from the bible and other various ancient texts say the same thing. We are from a Power greater than us Who is made up of Light, and we belong back with that loving Presence in the end. They are also saying we must work through karma, let go of material desires and egoistic goals to reach that Divine Creator. We're also told that loving Ascended Masters such as Jesus, Buddha, and Krishna are not just for certain people who belong to certain denominations but also for all souls as there's no real separation. The only delusion of separation that's there is the one that man creates.

As I stated in the beginning of this chapter, there's just so much more I could say on this subject, but in the spirit of keeping things simple, I will end it with this final excerpt. It's from the Big Book of Alcoholics Anonymous in the chapter to the Agnostic, page 46. In my opinion, I think it sums it all up perfectly, and if there's one thing I want you to remember about the spiritual path, it's this:

"We found that God does not make too hard terms with those who seek Him. To us, the Realm of Spirit is broad, roomy, all-inclusive; never exclusive or forbidding to those who earnestly seek. It is open, we believe, to all people."

VISUAL SIGNS
& EVIDENCE

Mind-blowing captures & miraculous signs.

AS EXCITING AS IT IS to capture audio responses from the other side, there's something really special about capturing visual evidence. Each capture is like a unique gift that I cherish greatly. I've noticed when it comes to skeptics or naysayers, they like to contest the audio even though a lot of the responses are clear and undeniable. But when they see visual evidence in the videos where most of my captures happen, they don't know what to say. It's hard to deny what they're seeing, yet they're so stuck in their beliefs, they say nothing of the visual evidence and attack something else. When believers get to see these photos, for them, it's just more confirmation there's an afterlife. I know that even though I'm the one who's had the honor of capturing these orbs, apparitions, and signs, it's my responsibility to share them with you. These gifts are not just for me; they're for everyone.

I will state this again just to make sure I'm clear, none of the photos you see here, on my website, or on my channel have ever been doctored or photoshopped in any way. The only thing I have ever done is adjust the contrast on a few of them to see something more defined. But most of these photos are just snapshots from videos on my channel. All of these photos can be seen better through the suggested links or on my website.

Let's take a look at some of the light anomalies I capture while doing sessions. I believe these to be true orbs and not dust, water droplets, or bugs. These different-sized orbs move in intelligent ways and arrive at certain times. They show up when asked and seem to be helpful. Some have entered and left my body while doing the sessions, and it's quite remarkable.

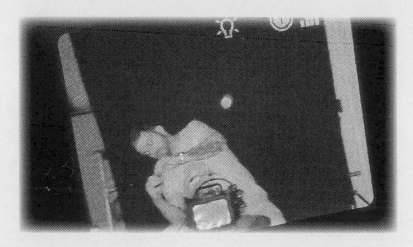

In the photo above, you can see a perfect orb near me as I conduct a spirit box session using the Portal. I use a black backdrop, so it's easier to spot these amazing balls of light when I review the footage.

In this photo, I'm sitting in my car at a cemetery as I do from time to time. I will go and sit there and intuitively connect to whoever I feel is looking for help. The amazing responses I've captured at these cemeteries are very powerful and telling. I don't believe souls just stay there, but I believe it is a place they visit if they're looking for help. You can see this perfect ball that just left my head moving straight up. They will often enter or leave around the region where my third eye, the pineal gland, is located, which is directly behind my forehead. [34]

Here I'm practicing my Kriya Yoga lying on my mat with my head slightly raised. You can see that I've got company to my left—another perfect ball of light.

These next set of photos are also very special. I was doing a session one night and speaking to my guru Paramahansa Yogananda, whom I will share more about later in the book.

---

[34] Watch a quick clip and another full video with orbs exiting my head at HOPEparanormal.com/video Video #12 &13.

But in the session, I invited him to visit, and you can see in the video, a bright visible ball of light comes down and turns and enters my back. This was one of the wildest captures I've ever recorded.

What are these balls of light? In my opinion, even though I'm not completely sure, I feel they are angels and souls that have ascended to higher levels of consciousness. Whether they are loved ones, spirit guides, or divine beings, I believe they are benevolent and are there to help. From what we've been told in ancient texts, from what the spirits have said, from what I've captured visually, we come from light and are made of it. Seeing these orbs move on camera is quite remarkable, and I urge you to watch the suggested links to my videos.

People over the years have asked me about children and what happens to them after death. The answer I give them is, I'm not sure. I have received many messages that the children

I've asked about were okay, and in the light with God. But there have been select cases where a child chose to stay behind for different reasons.

Here I'll show you two photos where I captured children in them. In this first photo, I am sitting in my chair conducting a session, and in the bottom right corner, the face of a young girl appears.

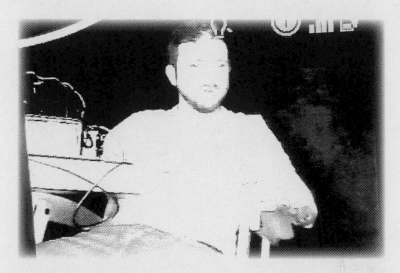

You can see her face with two eyes, nose, and mouth. In the session I was doing, I was hearing children coming through.[35]

---

[35] Watch the full session at HOPEparanormal.com/video Video #14.

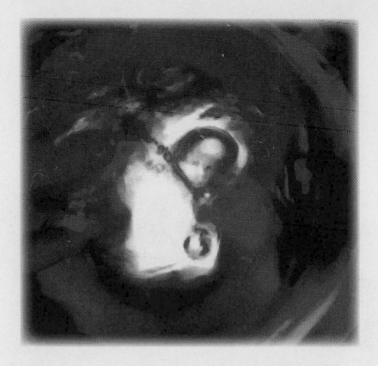

This is a remarkable picture of a young child Nikki and I captured years ago. This was captured doing water ITC, a technique where you use a bowl of water and light directly underneath or above it. With your hand, you agitate the water and snap photos asking for the spirit to show themselves. In this case, we captured what looks like a baby swaddled in a cloth. Still blows my mind after all these years.

This next photo below is one of the most important I've ever captured and is a still shot from a video. What you see in this photo actually happens in the sky right before your eyes, the best kind of proof. I had just received my first Panasonic DR60 voice recorder and was at the cemetery. I was saying a prayer for the spirits there and mentioned Jesus Christ. The second I did, a cross appeared in the clouds above me. I never noticed it until a wonderful subscriber saw it and messaged me. The photo sits on my desk today as a constant reminder the Lord is there. This was undeniable.[36]

And now I will share what may be the most important picture I've ever snapped. There's so much in this photo, but one image within it makes it impossible to deny. When I took it, I was out in my backyard on the phone with a client giving her a reading. She asked to speak with her grandmother, and I was able to connect pretty well with her. I was getting that she had met Jesus and knew He was always there even when she didn't see Him. Something told me to look up, and when I did, I saw an eye looking at me. I thought it was weird; I snapped a photo and went back to the call. Later I remembered and checked the photo; this is what I captured.

---

[36] See the cross form in the video at 5:03-5:11 at HOPEparanormal.com/video Video #15.

At first glance, you may not see much, or you may see the eye that I saw. To me, it appears to be Jesus as I see the shape of his head, nose, and beard. Slightly above his forehead is what appears to be a dove flying up, and above that, I see a lion's head. Now maybe you have to use your imagination, or maybe you see it right away. In case you can't fully visualize it, let me show you my rendering.

Hopefully, you can see what I saw but take a look below Jesus's head around where His heart would be. An unnatural shape appears to be there, and it resembles the Life Piece, the design Connie channeled when I asked Jesus what it was He used to make. You can see the shape as clear as day in the original but let me blow it up for you a bit.

As you can clearly see, a small circular design with lines running out from it to another larger circle is visibly there. You may have to use your imagination with the other visions I described, but you don't have to imagine seeing this remarkable design. This photo was taken on April 16th, 2019, during Holy week. Again what's wild about this photo, I saw Jesus, the dove, the lion but never saw the Life Piece design. It wasn't until the client I was giving the reading to saw it after I had sent it to her. It's amazing when other people are seeing these signs, and it's not just me.

This image will now lead us right into the next chapter discussing the significance of the Life Piece.

THE LIFE PIECE

So much meaning in one little design.

I'VE ALREADY SHARED WITH YOU how we came to know about the Life Piece.[37] The connection I felt to it the moment Connie channeled it was incredible. I didn't realize that I was going to discover that this simple little design wasn't as simple as I had originally thought. I think even more will continue to be revealed in the years to come.

Now before I go into these other connections I've uncovered so far about the Life Piece, I would like to express a thought. Many have said Jesus was a gnostic. The word gnostic comes from the Greek word *gnosis*, meaning knowledge, but not primarily rational knowledge, more so intuitive knowledge.

In 1945, in Nag Hammadi, Egypt, a great discovery of ancient scrolls was made in a cave. They were hidden in a cave because the Fathers of the early Church wanted them destroyed as they considered them heresy. Among the texts found were the gnostic gospels of Thomas and John. Again denounced by the Catholic Church after being found, they were not accepted as true scripture. Many of the writings use Christian terminology, unmistakably related to a Jewish heritage. They claim to offer traditions about Jesus that were secret and hidden from many people that considered themselves in the second century to be Orthodox Christians. These Orthodox Christians believed Jesus to be the Son of God uniquely distinct from the rest of humanity for whom He is the Savior. Yet in the Gospel of Thomas when

---

[37] See story in chapter- *The Next Chapter*,-page 56.

Thomas recognizes Jesus, Jesus tells him they both came from the same Source. He says to Thomas,

> *"I am not your master. Because you have drunk, you have become drunk from the bubbling stream which I have measured out… He who will drink from my mouth will become as I am: I myself shall become he, and the things that are hidden will be revealed to him."*[38]

Jesus had a way of speaking that even His simplest of words had a deeper meaning. This is quite evident in both the bible and the Gospel of Thomas, including when He speaks to me intuitively. I don't know how many times He would say something simple to me, and it wasn't until later on that I truly understood what He meant.

> Matthew 6:22, KJV, *"The light of the body is the eye: if therefore thine eye be single, thy whole body shall be full of light."*

If we look at this verse, many have understood this to be Jesus saying if we see and perceive good things with our eyes, if we are generous and caring, then our Godly purpose becomes our sole vision for our lives, and we become more like God. Now even though that interpretation is meaningful and isn't wrong as far as making sense, there is yet a deeper meaning. The pineal gland, known as the third eye, located behind the forehead, is believed to be the spot where the soul enters and leaves the body at birth and death. In meditation, when we turn our gaze up and in, almost crossing our eyes, we direct our vision to become one through the third eye. This focuses attention through that one single point in meditation, we are knocking on Heaven's door, and the light will appear.

---

[38] Gospel of Thomas - Verse 13 & 108.

Once we are able to walk into that light, our bodies are filled with God's energy, and we are illumined. This is the ultimate goal that can be achieved while we are still alive. The sayings, "heaven on earth," "a death before dying," and "the kingdom of God is within us" all have deeper meanings than the surface interpretations we are given in Sunday service from our pastor. Christ was guiding us somewhere more meaningful.

I share this because the Life Piece's meaning is remarkable and is a true guide for how to live our lives, but there's something else even bigger. First, let me show you the full diagram of the design with the 14 inner and outer qualities of the self listed.

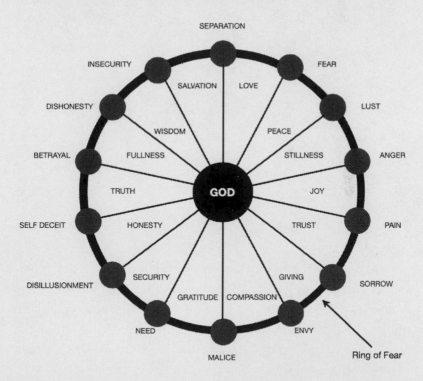

We begin at the God dot, and because we become so attached to the physical life we lead here on earth, our egos take over. This is fear-based thinking, which is what those lines running away from God represents. That brings us to the "ring of fear," where we continue on a viscous cycle living in our outer qualities, which aren't very good. The only way to get back to God is through our inner qualities that point us right back to Him. It's that simple and amazing. The shape of the piece is half of a sphere with the God dot at the top. The way the Life Piece is shown in its 3D model, it reveals a descending and ascending action that takes place for us.

We see that there is a pretty powerful purpose for the design and what it means. Whether it came from Jesus or not, this alone is clearly an amazing reminder of how to stay on track in our lives. But let's look further. One of the first things I found, marking the place believed to be where Jesus Christ was born in Bethlehem, a 14-point star is mounted.

The significance behind this 14-point star in the grotto of the church of the Nativity in Bethlehem is to remind us of the genealogy of Christ. Matthew 1:17 NIV:

"Thus there were fourteen generations in all from Abraham to David, fourteen from David to the exile to Babylon, and fourteen from the exile to the Christ."

This I found to be very interesting and felt it somehow brought validation to the Life Piece as I had never seen a 14-point star associated with Jesus.

A couple of years later, I was given another piece of the puzzle, but this time in the form of science. I belong to a public group on social media where they conduct experiments in cymatics. Cymatics merges the fields of sound, geometry, light, and mathematics through images created by all frequencies. In this group, it's not uncommon to see videos where a certain frequency is being piped into a speaker underneath a basin of water or a table with sand. The vibration from the sound creates geometric designs in the water or sand, revealing what these frequencies actually look like. One of the first examples of this I had ever seen was Steve Halpern, a musician, using a soundtrack of himself chanting OM in one of the great pyramids. The results proved that vibration manipulated matter.[39]

One day looking through countless videos in the group, I came across a frozen standing wave created with the frequency of 111Hz.

I couldn't believe my eyes. There it was, the Life Piece. The same design given to us by Jesus through Connie's channeling. The same 14 points on the star that marks the supposed place of Jesus's birth. The same design that appeared in the clouds with what looks like Jesus above it. So why is this so significant? Because this was the design that showed up when 111Hz was played. This

---

[39] Watch this video at HOPEparanormal.com/video Video #16.

frequency is known as the "Divine" or "Holy" frequency. Yup, you read that right. How amazing is that?

There are several ancient megalithic sites all over the world that resonate at frequencies between 95Hz-120Hz. The Maltese Hypogeum, an ancient temple carved out from rock some 11 meters underground, dates back to 3500BC. This temple was not only built to serve as a sacred place for spiritual practice but also to resonate at exactly 111Hz. But why?

When an extensive study was done on ancient architectural acoustic resonance patterns and brain activity, the frequencies 110Hz-112Hz had a unique effect on the brain.[40] The brain's activity lowered and moved from the prefrontal cortex, deactivating the language center and temporarily switching from left to right-sided dominance. This is the most highly evolved part of the brain responsible for intuition, creativity, empathic perception, and self-conscious awareness.

This means that the Life Piece is not only an absolutely beautiful representation of the ebbs and flows of the soul's spiritual journey, it's also an actual picture of the exact "Divine" frequency that scientifically unlocks the highest evolved part of the brain. The part of the brain that controls the sixth sense, intuition.

Jesus Christ not only gave us the design for living; He also gave us the actual key to help unlock it.[41]

---

[40] Information from "Ancient Architectural Acoustic Resonance Patterns and Regional Brain Activity" - By Ian A. Cook, Sarah K. Pajot, Andrew F. Leuchter.
[41] Watch the video where I discuss this photo and the LifePiece at HOPEparanormal.com/video Video #17.

INFLUENTIAL PEOPLE

People that have inspired me in what I do.

CONNIE FOX

CONNIE FOX HAS BEEN SUCH a big part of my journey, I feel it's important that I share a little bit more about this amazing person. One day early on, when we were meeting up at different locations, I asked her about when she got her ability. She told me at age 21, with friends at a club, she decided to go to the ladies' room. Inside the stall, of all places, she heard an internal voice, very calmly say, "Hello, Connie." Freaked out, she asked, "Who is this?" The voice answered back, "I'm one of your angels, and I'm here to support you."

Shortly after, she heard the voice again and decided to start telling her friends, family, and even boyfriend about it. But like many intuitively gifted people, she was met with resistance. Not wanting to be looked at like she was crazy, she ignored it and decided not to bring it up again. Connie being a very beautiful woman, was a model in addition to becoming a successful real estate investor, and it wasn't long before she got engaged to the man of her dreams. With a good size savings, a beautiful home, and a promising future, it all came to a crashing halt when she got a debilitating illness.

Bedridden due to mercury poisoning and Lyme disease, she suffered from a slew of health problems over the course of eight years. In that time, she lost her savings, fiancé, and even had to sell her home to pay for her medical expenses. During that period, she had been suffering greatly and decided to muster up the courage to ask for Jesus. Once she asked, He immediately came to her.

After recovering enough to start trying to rebuild her life finally, she knew this time it would include this Divine gift she was given. Learning more about her illness and studying to become a Holistic Health Practitioner, she found a way to use her intuition to help others afflicted with the same and other difficult sicknesses. She began writing books and doing more consultations, helping people connect with their deceased loved ones.

Even though Connie had been aware of her gift and using it for twenty years by the time we met, I feel she was reaching yet another level of consciousness. What we all experienced during that time was just so powerful and was imprinted on all of our souls. In one of our sessions one night, Jesus had told us Connie and I were brother and sister in a previous life. That we had agreed to meet up in this life to continue our spiritual work. Now whether that's true or not, Connie has always felt like a true member of my family.

STEVE HUFF

Not only has Steve Huff been instrumental in my own ITC journey, but the field as a whole also wouldn't be where it is today without him. No one has been attacked and yet at the same time copied for their ideas in this field more than Steve Huff. He has dedicated the last ten years of his life to real spirit communication and developing better devices, at times giving away the schematics for free.

Steve, like myself, started out as someone who just wanted to find out the truth about the afterlife. He didn't realize he would have such a great connection to it. Over the years, it seemed like the responses he was receiving were getting clearer and clearer. Whenever he used a new box or tried a new method, I would do the same and get the same mind-blowing results. What I think is even crazier, a year before ever talking to Steve, I was told through Connie's channeling that he and I would become as close as brothers. Sure enough, that is what our relationship is like today. He is like the brother I never had, or at least in this lifetime.

As Steve and I continue to conduct sessions for ourselves and other people, we both experience these highs and lows when it comes to what it is we capture. Some sessions are absolutely amazing, while in others, barely anything will come through. Every other week when we catch up on the phone, we notice we are normally experiencing the same highs and lows around the same time. This has led both of us to believe that we have many of the same spirit guides helping us. Many of the same names have been mentioned, and we feel it explains the synchronicities we've had. Whatever it is, having someone to connect with when it comes to this unique work has been a real Godsend, literally.

Steve continues to dedicate his time to developing clearer communication, and there's no doubt the ITC field will continue to benefit from his further discoveries. Many now have publicly said it was him that first inspired them to try ITC for themselves. They too have found extraordinary results with some of them even starting channels of their own. My guess is, just like with myself, Steve will continue to be attacked and called a fake, but it seems to come with the territory. Through countless testimonies, we both know that there are many people who have truly been helped by what it is we do.

With Steve, he always says, "Love is the Key," and I couldn't agree with him more. He continues to be a beacon of light for both sides of the veil, and I'm blessed to call him a true brother of the Soul.[42]

DEBRA KATZ

Debra Katz's story is unique in a way as it certainly gave me hope. She explains that as a younger woman, she became a federal probation officer for ex-cons being released from prison. Being that it was a stressful job, she decided to go enroll in a beginners' meditation class. While she was there, she noticed a flyer for an intuitive development class. Debra enrolled, not knowing what to expect but quickly found out she had a powerful psychic connection. From there, she worked hard at developing her ability, and still, to this day, continues to do so.

What I find amazing is she understands that we all have an intuitive ability we can tap into, and she genuinely wants to help people reach that goal. Debra has now helped thousands of people as clients and students reach higher levels of consciousness with her teachings. God knew exactly who it was I needed as a teacher as everything she taught me is now the foundation of my intuitive practice. Each time I would hit some kind of psychic block, which happens from time to time, she has always been there to help. She even experienced something similar to what happened to me with Reverend George and the spiritualist church. She told me it took time for her to get over being duped, but eventually, she did.

Debra is a perfect example of someone willing to believe in themselves and then work hard to achieve her goals. She has worked with some of the most respected experts in their fields, founded the International School of Clairvoyance, and with her

---

[42] Watch the Huff n HOPE Documentary "Finding the Light" at HOPEparanormal.com/video Video #18.

Master's Degree in Social Work, she recently got her Ph.D. in Psychology. When she hit obstacles, she worked through them, and that's one of the biggest things she teaches to her students. When encountering a block of some kind, she gently guides students to be patient and use the tools they were taught. She taught us we are powerful beings that don't even know our own strength, that if we did, we wouldn't dare doubt ourselves again.

One of the coolest moments with Debra I can remember, and there are many, she was giving me a personal reading over the phone before I began training with her. The information she was telling me was all very accurate as to what was going on in my life at that time. She knew very little about me and certainly didn't know anything about my connection to Jesus as I hadn't shared that with anyone yet. Debra, being three thousand miles away in California, abruptly says, "I see Jesus with you. You have this very strong connection with Him. It's like you have your finger on the Source somehow, almost like it's a button you're pushing." As she was saying this, I was holding my newly carved Life Piece, and without realizing it, my thumb was firmly pressing on the God dot.

CONNECTING INTUITIVELY

WORKING FOR A HUGE PSYCHIC NETWORK

ONE OF THE THINGS DEBRA warned her students about was going to work for one of those large psychic networks. She said anyone could do it with their ability, but she found those that did got easily burned out. Nikki and I were both anxious to start using our gifts and felt we were young enough; we could handle the rigors of being a practicing psychic medium. We had both practiced giving free readings for close to two years and felt it was time to start taking on real clients. We both decided to apply to one of the country's largest networks and hoped for the best.

Within a couple of weeks, we were interviewed by phone and moved on to the next stage of the hiring process. Stage two consisted of having to give short readings to two of the network's employees. We passed that stage with flying colors, and just like that, we were both hired. We were to receive a percentage of what the client paid for the call and could work our own hours. We were both very excited.

I would log on during the day, and Nikki would log on at night. We were both giving readings to about ten to fifteen people a day, four days a week. The length of time each call would last would range from fifteen minutes to an hour and a half. The majority of the people calling in wanted to ask about their love lives and had no interest in other topics. But every ninth caller or so, there would be one who was honestly looking for some spiritual guidance or wanted to speak to a deceased loved one. Those were the calls that made taking the other excruciating ones worth it.

Ultimately, the information Nikki and I were giving to the clients was accurate and helpful. We were constantly rated by the clients on a number of different categories, and accuracy was definitely one of them. Our ratings were some of the best in the company, and those that had excellent ratings were flown out to California as a token of appreciation. It was nice to be recognized for our performance, and we enjoyed the experience very much.

But just like Debra warned, the load of tapping into all of these people each day started to take its toll on both of us. We noticed after almost two years, we were logging in less and less. It's important to have a solid meditation and grounding practice to cleanse yourself each day when doing this type of a rigorous energy work, and even though I did, it still got to be too much. I remember, one day, a woman got on the line and only had about ten minutes she could afford to talk and wanted to speak with three of her deceased loved ones. Instead of telling her no, that it would be too much for me to do, I used the request as an opportunity to see if I could reach all of her loved ones. Each person she asked for by their first name only and I successfully gave her an accurate description of each person. I've had many memorable calls while working for this network, but that was one I'll never forget.

Eventually, Nikki and I both put in our two weeks' notice, but working there taught me a lot. In that time, I had given over fifteen hundred readings between the network and my own private clients. I had seen how when I trusted my ability and Higher Power I was 90% accurate or better. If I was in a bad mood for whatever reason or distracted by other life responsibilities, I wasn't as accurate. I realized Debra was right and no one should be reading that many people each day. After quitting the company, I continued my ITC research. The only readings I gave from that point on were the type I loved to give: spiritual guidance and connecting people with a deceased loved one.

Nikki, on the other hand, was so burned out from working there that she took a four-year hiatus and within the last year just started getting back into her practice. The biggest lesson I got from that whole experience, listen to your teacher.

WHAT WE CREATE IN OUR MINDS TRULY EXISTS

A thought-form is a radiating and floating form made up of energy that consists of mental and emotional matter. In layman's terms, what we create in our minds can actually exist in some shape or form in another dimension. So, if I create a red bouncy ball in my mind, somewhere in the spirit realm, the ball is there. Being taught this, one has to wonder, how real could it be? I figured, it's a nice notion, but there's no real way of proving this theory to be true.

One night, Nikki received a phone call from a family friend back in Ohio. The woman shared with Nikki that her 13-year-old daughter was having some issues and was a bit hesitant to discuss the situation. The woman told Nikki she had found out through the family that both of us were able to deal with paranormal matters and hoped we could help her. She explained that her daughter saw a half-man, half-creature in her room, who told her to take a belt and hang herself in the closet with it. The woman not knowing what to do, called a psychiatrist, who recommended she bring the girl in for a seventy-two-hour psych evaluation. Well, she did just that and while the girl was there, started to feel bad for not believing her daughter. That's when she decided to call Nikki and ask if there was anything we could do to help.

Based on my experience when it came to dealing with negative energies in the past, I felt we could at least try and help. But instead of doing an "in-person" cleansing, it would have to be a remote intuitive session like when Nikki first saw Christ in a field. So, the next night while the girl was still in the psych ward, Nikki and I sat in our chairs out back and prepared to attempt a cleansing remotely. We both got quiet, and I repeated the girl's name to myself and watched the vision of her house unfold. There I was standing inside her home in a dark hallway. The plan was, I was to fight whatever it was and Nikki would focus her energy as back-up.

Quickly, I noticed movement down the hall as if a dark figure was watching and moving about, but not in plain sight. Once I noticed that, I envisioned reinforcing my body with armor similar to what a knight would wear. As I walked down the hall, I felt like I was really there. In reality, I was sitting in my backyard with my eyes closed, but in what felt like virtual reality, I was walking down a dark hallway toward who knows what. As I passed doorways to different rooms, I heard noises. Whatever this thing was, it knew I was there. I had never done this before and was just going off what I was seeing and feeling.

Before I knew it, what seemed to be part-man, part-reptile attacked me from the side and it was on. What transpired for the next twenty minutes was like something you'd see in a Marvel super-hero movie. I would land punches and knock it down only for it to get back up, hide, and attack me again. I used a slew of techniques, including grounding it, keeping it from running off, but it would break free, making it difficult. There were times it would get the upper hand until I could envision a better line of defense, such as another weapon or reinforced armor. Eventually, I told Nikki I was getting tired and needed to do something else. Finally, in a last-ditch effort, I called out to Jesus Christ for help, telling Him that I did all I could to help and asking Him for guidance. Right then, Christ in all white was there next to me and held me. At that moment, white light shot out of Jesus's body in all directions like a light grenade and the body of this entity got blasted out of the house. Like that, it was over.

The next day, the girl was released from the hospital with the doctors saying there was nothing wrong with her that they could find. One of the doctors even delicately suggested it could be a spiritual matter, which shocked me greatly. From that point to current day, now age twenty, the girl has never had another incident like that again and remains problem-free. Now, I can't tell you for a fact that everything I envisioned that night really happened, but whatever did happen resulted in a positive outcome. Whatever we did that night and at many other people's haunted homes throughout the years was somehow effective.

Years after that particular experience, I was doing a session in my back room as no one was home and had the house to myself. I had all my different gear set up and wanted to see if any spirits were looking for help. I turned on the Portal and began envisioning a room in the astral dimension. The room had a door, a table, and the Portal sitting on top of it. I walked over to the door, opened it, and there were a number of souls looking to come in. As I'm describing this, you can hear the spirits mention what it is I'm seeing. I see about fifteen spirits coming into the room and a spirit says, "There's too many." I then envision putting out chairs for them to sit in and immediately one of the spirits mentions sitting in one of the chairs. I tell them that I'm calling on an angel to come and help, and a spirit says, "That's why I'm sitting here." I couldn't believe it.

It was such a profound experience, I named the video Mind-Blowing Session.[43] It truly was a breakthrough as it proved that the "thought-forms" I had created in my mind were indeed real, and the spirits could interact with these objects. But then something else happened. Something that would be the beginning of a long and difficult saga involving a troubling spirit. As the spirits were receiving light, someone came in and shut the door. A voice is then heard saying, "Frank... he's shutting the door," and you literally can hear the sound of a door being shut. Once I heard this, I ordered this Frank to stop, but it wasn't immediately clear if it was effective.

The whole story behind this Frank character is a wild one, possibly the craziest I've experienced in all my time of doing this work, but I'm saving that for another chapter. The most important thing to take away from these stories is that there is proof we truly can create another reality with our minds. It's been said in the book already, and I'm sure I'll mention it again, we are powerful beings that have no idea what we're truly capable of.

ASTRAL PROJECTION

Astral projection is a term used to describe an intentional out-of-body experience. This is different from remote viewing, where someone would visually see a place separate without essentially leaving their body. Astral projection is actually leaving the body temporarily as a soul and being able to explore different places. I experimented with three different people, where I attempted to

---

[43] Watch this mind blowing session at HOPEparanormal.com/video Video #19.

visit them in spirit and see if they would be able to consciously remember what it is I did when I showed up.

I asked a client, Steve Huff, and my friend, Chris, to participate. The way this would work, I would tell the person, to focus on a door before bed and see me standing there. Then to ask their spirit guides and angels to allow me to visit them. I told them nothing else. While they slept, I would meditate in my chair and perform the technique of leaving my body and go visit them. Once there, I would do something simple, such as touching their hand or foot, then leave. Upon waking up, if the person was to remember what it is I did, they would know within the first few moments.

So, the first person was my client. A very kind married woman, who had gotten a few readings from me in the past. She was interested in intuitive development, and I thought she would be perfect for this experiment. Trying it with three different people all over the country would truly give me a chance to see what would happen. I gave the client her instructions, and late that night, when I knew she'd be asleep, I sat down, focused on the client, and began the process. It wasn't long before I was flying through the air and landed outside of a house. I walked through the front door and the first thing I noticed was a dog, a black lab that lifted his head as if he'd noticed me come in. I looked around and found her room and entered. Inside the room, she and her husband slept in the bed with another dog near the foot of it. Without trying to be a creeper, which at this point was pretty much impossible, I went over to her side and saw a tattoo on her ankle. I couldn't make out what it was but decided that would be the spot. I lightly tapped my hand on her ankle, where the tattoo was, turned around and went back out the front door.

The next day, I woke up to a text telling me that when she woke up she instantly knew I had touched her right ankle, no question. I then asked her if she had a tattoo and, sure enough, there was a small green dolphin right where I saw it. I was so happy it worked and she was absolutely amazed. I wasn't as surprised anymore, rather just excited I could do something like this, that it was possible.

Next, I gave Steve the same instructions, and later that night when I knew it would be a good time, I visited him in Arizona where he lived at the time. I went over to his bed, saw his wife, Debby, and because Steve shaves his head and is bald, I felt that was a good target. I tapped the top of his head a few times and left. The next morning, a text from him read "I felt something around my head area." Success again.

With Chris, I wanted to try something a little different on my end. The instructions for him were the same, but this time I was going to try and exert more pressure when making contact with a part of Chris's body. So late at night, I sat in my chair and blasted off like a rocket out of my body. I entered Chris's house and saw his right arm hanging off the bed. I floated over and grabbed his wrist and with both hands twisted. I grew up with Chris and he always had a couple of years on me. Sometimes he used to rough me up so this was just a little friendly payback.

The next morning, I received a text from Chris letting me know I grabbed his right wrist and there was a red mark on it. He sent me a picture and, sure enough, there was a distinct red mark where I envisioned grabbing him. This would explain how in certain haunted situations, people can get scratched or grabbed. There would literally be no difference in that and in what I did to Chris.

This was all the proof I needed. Three separate times I tried it, and each time it worked. What I love about the findings in this experiment is that the evidence is conclusive. Each participant gave me the correct, specific answer with no way of knowing that information unless it happened on some level. It's that simple. I get it; for most people, these claims are not easy to just accept. But again it shows, the reality we perceive is far from what the ultimate reality actually is.

TELEKINESIS IS REAL

Telekinesis is another topic that most people don't know the truth about. Heck, I was one of them. Telekinesis, also known as psychokinesis is the psychic ability allowing a person to influence a physical system without physical contact. I honestly had no idea what to believe when it came to moving stuff with one's mind. I've always loved the idea of becoming a real Jedi like Luke Skywalker. The only way I knew to find out if something was real or not was to test it and that's exactly what I did. Well, let me tell you, just like creating thought-forms and traveling outside of one's own body, moving stuff with the mind is very real.

A company in the UK sells a small wheel that moves according to someone's energy level. I saw a couple of people in videos on YouTube holding their hands up to it without touching it, and the wheel was moving on its own. How though? Static electricity? Heat? If you remember my first Ouija experience, the planchette moved on its own throughout the night. Even though a spirit might have been communicating at that time, it was mainly our energy helping to move that plastic piece. I also explain in the chapter "Hard to Believe" how our intentions are constantly leaving our bodies, going into the universe through light particles. Well, the same is happening when it comes to telekinesis. The life force energy known to move physical objects telepathically has been called Chi.[44]

I ordered the wheel and once it arrived I pulled it out and set it up on my desk. I turned on my camera and began testing. I held my hand up to it like they did in the videos and, sure enough, it moved in one direction. I held my other hand up to it, and it began turning in the opposite direction, which was interesting. That would indicate a flow of energy like a magnetic field of some kind. I then moved away from it about six feet and began focusing my attention on it turning in one direction, even stating out loud which direction I wanted it to move. It started moving in the desired direction, which could still have been a fluke. So I said out loud, which helps with intention, to stop and begin turning in the opposite direction. Well, wouldn't you know, it did just that.

I continued to practice using the wheel for the next few days and got considerably better as I was able to replicate the same results over and over. Sometimes I was able to get the wheel to spin even faster than I did in previous tries. But then I went on to YouTube and found a guy using tin foil, match sticks, and spoons as the items he was moving. So, I put the wheel off to the side and created a little setup, where I stuck a needle standing up in an eraser with a piece of bent foil resting atop. I then put a huge, clear plastic bowl over all of it to rule out any draft or my breath interfering with the experiment. I focused just as I did with the wheel, and after about ten minutes of intently focusing on the foil moving in a specific direction, it began to move.

---

[44] Chi is the energy of life itself, a balance of Yin and Yang, positive and negative, electromagnetic energy, which flows through everything in creation.

Again and again, I was able to replicate the same results moving the foil in each direction I intended.[45] For me, this was just another example of how we've been told something isn't real and yet if we do the proper research and dedicate the time, the truth will reveal itself. After these experiences with creating astral objects, traveling through astral realms, and moving physical objects with my mind, I sent away for a certificate to become an honorary Jedi. I felt I'd earned it.

But just as easily as I was able to do those amazing things, I have hit many points in this journey, where I haven't been able to. I still have this fear that one day I will wake up and my intuitive ability will be gone. I've been told by Debra and even Jesus intuitively that I will never lose my ability but the fear still exists. So, the best remedy for that I've found is humility and faith. Humility is needed because even though I have the right to provide for my family, this gift was awoken in me to help people. It's not to perform magic tricks on command to impress crowds. Faith is needed because regardless of whether or not I feel like the amazing soul/being of light that I am, I know deep down I'm always a child of God and just need to show up. The humility relieves me of the pressure I unnecessarily put on myself to perform and the faith reassures me I'm right where I'm supposed to be regardless of how I feel.

---

[45] Watch this video at HOPEparanormal.com/video Video #20.

THIS WORK CAN BE MESSY AT TIMES

THERE ARE PROS AND CONS in everything we do. It seems whether it's a passion or an occupation, there's a level of suffering everyone has to go through to succeed. My advice has always been, pick something you don't mind suffering for. Like anything worth doing in life, there are sacrifices one must make to achieve their goals. But those sacrifices should never come at the expense of anyone's wellbeing. So, when I'm asked what's the best advice to give someone looking to start this type of research themselves, I tell them to work on their personal connection with God first. That might seem like putting the cart before the horse for some who are looking for answers about God or the afterlife, but going into the spirit realm without some basic understanding of a Higher Power is like walking around New York City for the first time, blindfolded with no one to guide you. Surely, you would stumble into some wonderful places with new amazing people, but unwittingly you would certainly wander down some dark alleys.

A person doesn't have to entirely figure out who God is to do this research as none of us truly know. But showing some type of willingness to want to know the Creator is important. Anyone in the early stages of conducting spirit-box sessions will eventually hear something about God that will cause them to wonder. That wonder grows into a desire for the truth. The answers we ultimately seek are not found through a spirit box or EVP, but more so through prayer and meditation. The search for God is not an external one. As people say in Twelve Step programs, "it's an inside job." Everyone looks outside of themselves for something that has been within them the whole time.

Once some kind of attempt is made to connect with a Higher Power, then dabbling in paranormal and ITC research is safer. For me, what I have found is this work has had a positive impact on who I am. It's been life-changing and even though I don't solely rely on spirit communication for answers, I've been given so many amazing validations about God's existence and how I have an important role in this universe (we all do). But let's talk about some of the negatives that can crop up while doing what it is I do.

Of course, how someone is living their life plays a big role in what they experience while doing this. Let's say I started doing spirit-box sessions when I was in active addiction. I would've had negative energy around me and that might have attracted negative spirits at that time. But even someone who has faith and tries to live a good life to the best of their ability, such as myself, can still hit a number of different snags.

One of the biggest problems I see amongst novice researchers, and I've been guilty of this myself, is the misinterpretation of spirit messages. No one is going to get them 100% accurate all the time, so misinterpretations are going to happen. Ultimately, these captions are someone's best guesses. Some people take time to objectively review their sessions and you can tell. But if a person doesn't learn early on that it takes several reviews and slowing down audio to properly transcribe sessions, they will have a completely different narrative to what's actually taking place. It's when people treat what they initially think they hear as fact and act on it that it becomes dangerous.

This is where objectivity and faith in a Higher Power really make a difference. If someone hears something they think is negative, say a prayer and leave it alone for a day. The next time you go to listen, say another quick prayer for clarity and see if it says the same as what was heard the day before. In most cases, it won't. This is why I review sessions three to four times over several weeks before finalizing. It took me some time to finally understand that, though.

Another potential pitfall in doing ITC sessions is becoming too involved and dependent on the communication. Once someone has made a successful connection and starts receiving somewhat clear responses, it's hard not to immerse oneself into doing it more and more. As crazy as it seems, friendships are established, or in some cases, re-established with souls on the other side. When someone starts to understand they have connections with real people that aren't in this realm anymore, it's powerful. At one point in this journey, I found myself listening to clips for hours trying to figure out what was said and becoming a bit obsessed. I have heard responses right away and thought they said something evil or nasty only to find out later it wasn't what I had originally heard. So, there is a real balance needed when doing this, and it is why having a sound mind is extremely important.

In addition to being looked at as a crazy person by many, something else most people don't think about as being a deterrent when getting into this type of research is receiving hate from random strangers. Don't get me wrong, I get way more support and love than hate for what I do, but the true hater is a special type of person. First, I'll say I'm no celebrity, but when someone puts their life out there for anyone to see, they can expect a certain amount of judgment and critique. I understand that. Plus, I always say that if someone is a skeptic and wants to respectfully discuss any of this, I have no problem doing that all day with them. It's the ignorant, hate-filled attacks that can make this work difficult at times.

When someone with a strong belief is presented with new information that contradicts what they hold to be true, it causes something called cognitive dissonance. This is usually experienced as psychological stress and, according to the theory, when two ideas are not psychologically consistent with each other, people will go to extreme lengths to change them until they are. Dealing with contradictory ideas is mentally stressful and requires energy along with an effort to sit with those ideas that all seem true. Many people deal with dissonance by just believing whatever it is they want. It's a lot easier for them. As Paramahansa Yogananda used to say, the perfect answer for these types of people is, "I'm sorry you feel that way, I bow to your colossal ignorance." I'm still working on responding with just that and nothing else after it.

There is one last drawback to communicating with spirits, whether that be through intuitive means or through ITC devices, and that is disruptive spirits interfering. It's not common, but it is a reality nonetheless. Notice I didn't say evil or demonic spirits. Why? Because even though those exist, the majority of spirits being negative or disruptive are spirits that have unresolved issues and can't cross. Just like I mentioned in the paragraph above, I receive hate from random people because they feel my work, my videos, my testimony somehow threatens to destroy their world. Well, it's no different with stuck, negative spirits, and however they were when they were alive, they will also be the same in death.

The problem with dealing with this same kind of negative people but in spirit form is that now we're not able to see them so easily. But this is where having a personal relationship with your Higher Power takes care of the issue. Having that connection or at least working on it gives you an actual aura of light protection, not to mention help from other angelic guides. I'm starting to sound like a broken record, as you can tell. My answer for mostly everything is God, yet this doesn't make it any less true. The protection we get from God is a fact based on the intuitive confirmations I've received and the audio recordings I've captured. So, just like running into a negative person at work or anywhere else, we will occasionally deal with a negative soul from time to time.

In all the sessions and readings I've done, the majority of them have been clear of any disruptors. Most messages I receive are positive and loving. I've been doing this for some time now and I can tell you, when someone negative is coming through, they will tell you. Someone will tell you. The idea that every voice is a demon, whether it's nice or nasty, is a crazy one and is based on the belief that the dead know nothing and that there isn't anything between heaven and hell. Hopefully, by now, I have shown you how those beliefs are very misguided.

This next story, though, is pretty wild and details one of the greatest spiritual challenges I've faced while doing this work. It served as a valuable lesson that not only continues to teach me how to deal with negativity on the other side but also in my own life.

THE ODD COUPLE

One day, I was sitting in my office when I saw my neighbor, Buddy, walk across the street and knock on my door. I answered it, and he informed me I had a tile on my roof starting to come loose. We went out into the middle of the street so I could see this dislodged piece of my roof, and, while standing there, just two neighbors having a friendly conversation about home repairs, I asked Buddy how long he's lived on the street. He told me he bought his home in the early 1980s, but couldn't remember who moved in first. I asked him what he meant, and he told me he didn't know if the woman who originally owned my home was there before him or not. I was curious about the history of my house but never enough to search for records or anything. I asked him what the woman's name was and with a gentle smile, he said the name, Alma. Every hair on my body stood up at that moment. I immediately asked if Alma had red hair and Buddy looked at me a bit confused and said, "Yeah, how did you know that?" I just stood there silent, at a loss for words. That's when Buddy said to me, "What's the matter? You look like you've seen a ghost."

As I stood there with this man that I may have had three conversations with in all the ten years I've lived there, I thought about that amazing night in the garage with Nikki. My first psychic vision was of a kind, red-haired woman named Alma. Nikki told me this woman was someone, who had spoken to her and was nice but didn't know who she was. Over the years once in a while Alma's name would come up, sometimes in a session. To me, this was amazing. There was no way this was just a coincidence.

Once I snapped out of my flashback, I asked Buddy about Alma some more, as in what she did, what she was like. He told me their families were close and would have dinner at each other's houses all the time. That she was a stenographer who taught piano and lived in the house alone. I asked if she ever had a husband, and Buddy told me she did, but that he didn't live there for long. He couldn't remember his name but could remember he was a huge asshole. Again the hairs started to raise on my body.

"His name wasn't Frank, was it"? I asked.

Buddy again looked at me, this time without the little smile he had before, and said, "Yeah, that was him."

In a matter of moments, under the hot Florida sun, standing in the street with my neighbor, I found out the woman whom Nikki and I both saw eight years prior was the original owner of my house. In addition to that, I found out the man who first interfered in that important, mind-blowing session and continued to do so over the years was Alma's ornery husband, Frank. Ever since that one time, Frank would pop up on different occasions causing problems in my sessions. Just like in that particular session, everything would be going well, and then my guides would mention his name. Responses like, "Frank's mean," "He hates you, Josh," "He killed a girl," "He's trying to stop you from helping," and "He won't leave," were the regular replies when Frank showed up.

My first confrontation with him was one like the incident where I had to battle that negative entity remotely. Only with Frank, I took charge quicker and pictured punching him in his face and then dragging him off into the desert. There, I shackled him and left. In the sessions I did after that, Frank was gone, but the spirits mentioned he was in some kind of jail. After hearing these types of validations, I felt that what I did was effective in removing him.

But with him something was different. A few months would pass, and, out of nowhere, Frank came back. The guides would always make it known when he did, and I would begin my next plan of attack. Again, when it was time, I would focus on him, forcing a confrontation of some kind only for him to disappear and then resurface months later. Every time I would face him, I would change my approach a little bit but nothing worked in keeping him away for good.

Buddy asked me how I knew Alma and Frank's names as well as her hair color. Without telling him any of what I've just shared with you, I told him that Nikki and I both had felt the presence of these two people. I left it at that but being the great neighbor Buddy is, he called me into his house to show me a couple of things he thought I might find interesting.

Sure enough, as I stood in his little home office looking over his shoulder at his computer screen, there she was. A picture of Alma smiling sitting at a table. One of the main things that stuck out was her red hair. Then, without saying anything, Buddy opened another screen and started typing away on his computer landing on a county records website. Before I could figure out what he was doing, I see Frank and Alma's names next to my address as the original owners of my house. Buddy was able to pull up the records from the old deed proving definitively these two people, whom Nikki and I had no formal knowledge of whatsoever, were the first owners of my house. For me, this was one of those moments, and I've had a few, where it truly proves without a doubt all of this is real.

After I had the facts and knew exactly who these people were, it made perfect sense. Frank was an old cantankerous drunk, who had been separated from his kind and caring wife, Alma. She stayed living in the house and he would come back to visit when he wanted. For whatever reason after death, this arrangement continued, and I somehow was caught in the middle of it. It became personal between Frank and me when I was inviting other spirits to come and communicate with me, and he didn't want them coming in "his" house. When I "Punched" him in the astral realm it became even more personal. I had no issue with Alma and thought of her as a kind woman, but she was the link in keeping Frank coming back each time. I knew I needed to do another session, which would've been my fourth up to that point.

The sessions I conducted were intense and powerful. Direct replies came through on both of them and an even clearer picture formed. Frank didn't want Alma to leave, and, on top of that, it seemed he had killed someone when he was alive, a young woman. I had no proof of that, but it was said numerous times through a spirit box or voice recorder. The fact that he was previously on the deed, I felt, made it harder to ban him from the premises for good. But again, after doing sessions to address both Alma and Frank, everything got quiet again.

One day, I got a piece of mail addressed to Alma, which was the first time anything like that had happened in the ten years I'd been living there. Shortly after, I was testing the small hacked radio, the Panabox, and Frank abruptly announced he was there. I got pissed, called him out, and one of the responses he said was "Get mad." This made sense as every time he got me upset, he would feed off that energy. So I knew I needed to be better than that. In the past, I wanted to deal with a situation like this with fighting, but it was starting to become clear I'd have to do this with compassion and understanding all the while still holding my ground.

With the family out of town for a week visiting Nikki's family in Ohio, I had the house to myself. I chose this time to conduct an all-out, final-stand type of session for Frank. I set up cameras and the portal in the main living room of my house, which I'd never done before. I wasn't going to get mad or fight him, I was going to speak to him and, if need be, call in the victim he murdered. I felt this would force him to face what he did and put him in a more vulnerable state. At that point, I would sit and focus on a direct stream of light hitting him until I felt it wasn't necessary.

Well, I did just that and the connection during the session was one of the best I had ever seen. Every response was a direct response to what I asked or said. Frank was there as were my guides, and when I called on the victim to show up, it very much sounded like she did. Frank was on the defense and wanted to leave, but I still focused light on him.

Afterward, the guides commented that Frank was gone. I will not fight Frank in the traditional sense again if he returns ever. I felt I was able to help Alma move on, but who really knows. All I know is there was a major difference after this crazy session I did. Frank taught me a lot. There were many attributes that he might have had that I did at one point in my life or in whose direction was heading. If I experienced redemption then Frank has the same opportunity. He may not take it, but who am I to judge him? I surely won't stand for anyone attacking me and my family in any way, but there's a great spiritual lesson here, and it's one of compassion, strength, and love. "Sinner or saint, I am Thy child" is true for everyone.

I'm sure there's more to understand with this whole ordeal as I'm constantly learning but the way I dealt with the "Franks" in the past compared to how I deal with them now has changed greatly. Who knows if I'll ever have to deal with him again, only time will tell. But whether it's Frank or someone else with or without a body, I will be ready to combat them with love. I may not always succeed at first, but it's my job to keep trying. I urge you to see the sequence of videos documenting the Frank and Alma saga.[46] It will surely captivate you.

---

[46] Watch this set of videos on Frank & Alma at HOPEparanormal.com/ video Videos #21, 22, 23, 24 & 25.

THE GURUS, GUIDES & ANGELS

A Divine team truly helps.

THROUGHOUT THE BOOK, I HAVE shared many different stories and examples of the powerful communication I've received from the other side. Now let me share with you a little bit about the amazing team that helps make it happen.

THE SPIRIT GUIDES AND ANGELS THAT HELP ME

When I first started working with the spirit boxes, I had no idea who was around or would help me. So, in each session, I would ask who was there and hope to get a name. I found I would get names in certain locations, but it wasn't until a couple of years in that I noticed hearing the name Bob in most sessions. Shortly after hearing his name, I started getting psychic hits on Bob, meaning I would get blips of information. I saw he was bald, he had glasses, and was some kind of engineer. I felt he worked on spirit boxes or with sound. I started asking for him in sessions and the spirits would say his name when he showed up. Once he did, the box would somehow work better. The spirits would even say he's working the box.

When I first started doing private box sessions for people in early 2018, I was booked up for a month straight doing five sessions a week. I still didn't realize how much energy it would take to do that many box sessions in such a short time. Throughout those sessions, I heard the guides getting frustrated. The quality of the responses in the sessions toward the end of the month started to wane as well. Now I only do one private session a week and take weeks off.

After doing those twenty private sessions in one month, I didn't hear from Bob again. I would still ask for him and certainly apologized for my ignorance, but Bob wasn't coming through anymore. I did hear a few responses referring to Bob dying or passing, and, of course, this made no sense to me. I'm still not completely sure about what happened to Bob, but years later, I discovered more information on how we're truly made up of a body, mind, and soul.

The way Swami Sri Yukteswar explained to his chela (student), Yogananda, when he visited him from the afterlife, we have a physical body and inside and around that body is an astral body. This astral body is also in the shape of a physical body, but includes what some call the aura, the energy field around us. It is in the astral body that we keep our memories (mind) and experiences that we take with us after the death of the physical body. Deep within the astral body is the causal body, which is our soul, and it is a bright ball of light. Yogananda talks of another death, but of the astral body this time. This death is not physically painful, but one that comes when a soul is ready to graduate to a higher sphere of consciousness or go back into a body. I can only guess this is what happened to Bob, as I didn't receive any more information on him, but I am eternally grateful for all his selfless contributions in all of this. [47]

Another amazing soul on the other side helping with all of this in more ways than I'll ever know is someone named Michael. Is he the infamous archangel that some of my followers seem to

---

[47] Watch this video from 2017 where I ask about Bob and Frank at HOPEparanormal.com/video Video #26.

think he is? Or maybe he's just a spirit guide in line for his wings. What I have received in psychic hits just like I did with Bob, was that Michael was someone who lived some time ago and lost his family in a fire. He had suffered great pain in his life, but his love for Christ carried him through. He then chose to devote his afterlife to service to the Father and at some point was sent to help me. I didn't consciously find out about Michael until I received the Panasonic DR60 voice recorder where communication advanced to another level for me. I will say though, when I went back through old sessions, there were replies in almost every one of them saying Michael's name. This led me to believe he had been there all along and, somehow, I felt I knew him previously.

Before I knew I even had a team of guides helping, I invited my friend, Adam, who was on the other side to help in the sessions. Here I was trying to hire a friend again just as I did in the past, yet this time it was in spirit, and little did I know, there was a dichotomy to how the team functioned. Bringing in someone who was still rough around the edges when it came to spiritual matters, even if they were in the spirit realm wasn't such a great idea. I found Michael and the others loved Adam and wanted to help him, but he still had a temper and would say things leading me to believe he wasn't ready to help just yet. So, I spent time working with Adam and felt progress was made, but he still had his own journey to go on.[48]

Michael seemed to be the lead guide that did most of the talking, yet there were others that I knew helped at different times. When Michael spoke, it was always strong and clear, plus his messages were always rooted in Christ's message with wanting to help others. One message I'll never forget that came through

---

[48] Watch a video on helping my friend Adam at HOPEparanormal.com/ video Video #27.

on the DR60 recorded was so powerful I don't think I could ever forget it. I asked if he had a message for the group while I was doing a session for people looking to reach their loved ones. His reply was, "The hard part of evolving, is fighting through the ascension. Help the masses come together." I took that message as a statement of how hard it can be to evolve, letting go of the ego that keeps us held down. Once we work hard to shed that part of us that doesn't serve us anymore, we can rise above it, we can ascend to higher levels of consciousness. Also, it's our job to help others do the same and collectively evolve.

All I could ever feel from Michael was love, but there came a time when I felt, like Bob, he too was doing too much. Because I had created such a great connection with him, I relied on him too much it seemed. He would suggest other guides could help, but I didn't always have the same results with them. In addition to being taxed with a heavy workload, Frank started messing with him. The way I understood it was, Michael had fully crossed into the light, but was a helper when it came to this work. He would have to travel through dimensions, and, when he was here, he was susceptible to spirits in this realm hence why Frank could affect Michael at times. It came to a point when Michael had to take some time off, and he disappeared.

For a while, I didn't hear from him on the recorder or through the box. The other spirits said he was gone and for me to find him. I would ask but get nothing, and finally I just accepted he needed to do whatever it was he was doing. He was a friend and a partner of sorts; I felt like I let my partner down by not being able to effectively deal with Frank. This is where the connection with Jesus made all the difference. The communication I was experiencing with these guides was advanced, to say the least. This wasn't just happening in my head; I had clear enough recordings that could be confirmed by many that these things were happening. At times, I felt myself worrying about them and even obsessed with trying to help more.[49]

I realized all I could do was pray for the safety of the guides that came through, hoping that no other spirit trying to disrupt the work we did was successful in doing so. I understood the guides were not at my beck and call, and didn't serve me like I was some master. If what I believed was true, we were all children of God trying to help where we could. I knew a lot of these same spirits were helping Steve too, as we would get many of the same names in our sessions. When Michael took a break from working with me, Steve wouldn't hear from him either. It felt like while we had our own obstacles to deal with on this side; they had their own stuff to deal with over there.

What I also noticed when it came to the guides, especially Michael, was that they were very blunt sometimes. I would receive very positive and supportive messages, but if I started doing something that wasn't conducive to my spiritual development, like missing meditation, not reading my spiritual material, getting too complacent or even lazy, Michael would let me know. At first, I would feel somewhat offended, but I learned to accept it as constructive criticism. It was Michael that first mentioned writing a book. Yes, I've always wanted to write one, but without the nudge, I probably wouldn't have started.

There came a time when I didn't know what else to do with this work. I prayed and asked Jesus for guidance, I asked for the answer in what my next move in all of this would be. A few days passed, and, suddenly, I felt compelled to start writing and begin planning events along with speaking engagements. It was like all of a sudden I had direction again. Once I received

---

[49] Watch a Video of me working with my guides and getting important answers at HOPEparanormal.com/video Video #28.

that information intuitively, Michael was mentioning the book in sessions. One morning, I woke up and while in the shower I was thinking of the daunting task of writing a book and what exactly I would write about. Suddenly, every one of these chapters just showed up in my head. Immediately, I turned the water off and scurried to a pen and paper and wrote them all down. Never had something like that happened before.

It was at this time that I reluctantly decided to go see a psychic that another one of my friends had recommended to me. After the Reverend George situation, I wasn't too keen on seeing anyone else's psychic. But I ended up going, and I'm glad I did. I was given such personal and accurate information I couldn't deny this woman had a gift. One of the many things she told me was that I was going to write a book and teach people about what was in it. Afterward, when I was leaving, I sat in my car and asked if any of the guides had a message. I recorded a loud response saying, "I'm so happy... all I wanted was for her to say this."

Over the next two years, the time it would take for me to write this book, life would get in the way at times as most of this was written during the 2020 pandemic. That meant there were periods I wasn't writing and when that happened, messages encouraging me to finish the book were constantly being heard. Responses such as, "Josh we're helping... finish the book. We'd still be working," which implied they couldn't resume regular sessions until the book was done. Another message showed me how invested the spirits were in all of this when I captured a response saying they were behind me, reading the book while I was writing it.

In addition to Michael, names such as Brian, Andrew, David, Lena, Betty, and Phillip have been repeatedly heard throughout past sessions. I believe these are the names of the guides that have helped throughout the years alongside many more that remain nameless. In addition to these wonderful and selfless souls, angels are constantly mentioned. One of the messages I've been given is that the orbs of light that are seen flying around are indeed angels bringing in light and helping. Many times I would intuitively see angels flying in and would announce their arrival. This is when responses would come through the box confirming what it was that I was seeing.

The fact is, even though there is still a lot I don't understand, I know without a doubt that true spirit helpers and angelic beings are assisting me. They truly care about what it is I'm trying to do. I wouldn't be able to do any of this work without them, and it's important they know I know that. When I think of all the sessions and videos that have been shown over the years, the people that have been helped, this book, and all that went into it, these are not just my accomplishments, they're ours. All of it has been done as a team. When someone messages me that a certain video helped them, or receiving a message from a deceased loved one changed their life, the guides and myself all had something to do with that. As a group, we ultimately chose to be humble servants of the Lord, and instead of me being some leader, I'm just a proud member of the team but on this side of the veil.[50]

It is also worth noting, some of the best communication I've ever captured was when I attempted to reach a few well-known people after their passing. Some of these people were celebrities that I felt a connection to and some were requested by the subscribers on my channel. Doing these types of sessions were seen as controversial because some thought it was just for views or that it was disrespectful, but nothing could be further from the truth. For the few celebrities I have asked for, there were many

---

[50] Watch a Video on Michael and my guides at HOPEparanormal.com/video Video #29.

more that people asked me to do that I didn't. Each session was always done with love and respect, plus I wasn't forcing anyone to come to the box. I'd ask, and if they had something they wanted to say, which 90% did, they would. It has now happened, where I have been conducting a session completely unrelated to anyone and a response comes through from the guides telling me a certain person would like to speak. A few times it has been a well-known person's name and when I asked for them, the results were astounding.

Now, I can't tell you that every person I asked for, the actual person really came and communicated with me. But if you watch these insanely powerful sessions, you can draw your own conclusions. I will just say that some of the responses in these sessions were some of the clearest, loudest, and most poignant responses I've ever heard in the eight years of doing this. So, with that said, people like Tupac Shakur, Jahseh Onfroy, Anthony Bourdain, Kobe Bryant, James Gandolfini, Chadwick Boseman, and many more hold a very special place in my heart.[51]

The fact that we can still carry on meaningful relationships with the people we loved that are no longer physically here, or that we can create new relationships with people we've never met is one that I'm extremely grateful for. If more people understood this reality, well, in the words of one of the guides coming through the box one night, "people wouldn't even be sad."

---

[51] Watch clips of well-known people I've reached out to at HOPEparanormal.com/video Video #30. If you wish to see more, I have a whole other playlist dedicated to sessions with celebrities on YouTube.com/HopeParanormalWhiteLight

THE GURUS THAT ARE
HERE TO HELP ALL

Back in 2013, when working with Connie regularly, I remember she channeled an enlightened Master named Muhavatar Babaji a few times. He sounded reserved and wise and spoke about breaking down the ego. I was intrigued but more interested in what Jesus had to say at the time. Even though I knew nothing about Babaji, I asked for him to come through shortly after Nikki got her ability. Nikki said he appeared in the lotus position, smiling, and simply said, "You are not ready for me yet." He then disappeared.

Skip to 2019, I decided to take the book the *Autobiography of a Yogi* off my bookshelf and began to read it. When I first saw Paramahansa Yogananda, I thought who is this long-haired fellow? But little did I know he would become my Guru and do so in a most spectacular way. Once I started reading his book, I realized I was reading it exactly when I was supposed to. They say, when the student is ready, the teacher appears. The fact that I had been through all I had in those six years and experienced so many spiritual happenings made all the difference. The evidence captured from my research was proof of life after death, real spirit communication, and the existence of God, and there I was beginning to read a book on the science of communicating with God.

Somehow I was drawn to classical Indian music and, while reading the book each day, I'd put on music by artists, such as Ravi Shankar and Nikhil Banerjee. Their songs contained ragas, which are a pattern of melodic notes used as a framework to improvise the music. The five notes that make up the ragas are said to have originated from Lord Shiva and have great power. I will say listening to this music helped me somehow truly absorb the stories Yogananda shared in the book. Sometimes a song would start and last the precise amount of time it took for me to read a chapter and felt like a perfect soundtrack. It was amazing as I can attest from personal experience there is true power in those notes.

Each day, I would read only about ten to fifteen pages as this allowed me to fully absorb what I was reading. Yogananda shares of his Guru Swami Sri Yukteswar, who had a Guru named Lahiri Mahasaya, whose Guru was Muhavatar Babaji. With each chapter being more captivating than the last, I was highlighting so much I thought my marker was going to run out of ink. So many holes were being filled in for me concerning the questions I still had about spirituality. Everything he was sharing in the book resonated as truth. But more than that I felt some kind of connection to this man. What's interesting about Yogananda is that he doesn't belong to any one religion. He honors all of them and loves Krishna, Jesus Christ, the Divine Mother, and the un-manifested Father. In most ashrams where they practice Kriya Yoga, an altar with pictures of all four Gurus along with Krishna and Jesus is present. An ashram is a spiritual hermitage or monastery.

In his book, he talks about how he grew up in India, and, even as a young boy, he searched tirelessly for a Guru to teach him how to reach God. When he finally found Sri Yukteswar, it was foretold to him that he would bring Kriya Yoga to the west and help many reach the Divine Creator. In time, the prophecy was fulfilled and he traveled to America, speaking all over the country. Eventually he founded the Self-Realization Fellowship, and centers began sprouting up all over the country and world. Today, there are millions of followers that practice Kriya Yoga as a means of attaining God-consciousness.

As I read more and more of the book, I saw Kriya mentioned a lot but nowhere does it show you how to actually do it. I looked online and even though there were small segments revealed, the whole process is protected and only open for those who are actually ready to receive the teachings. Yoga means union with God, and Kriya is a process of exercises, breathing, and meditation. It's honestly so much more, but for the sake of this book not ending up at 549 pages like the Guru's, I'll keep it short. Once I read where Kriya came from, how it was brought back into existence after the dark ages by Babaji, I felt called to learn it.

I couldn't fly out to the SRF Mother Center in Mt Washington, Los Angeles, so I was able to find an ashram in Miami where I'd get to physically learn the actual movements of Kriya. Even though I knew the process of fully learning it would take years, I was excited to start the journey. The initiation wouldn't be held for a few months as they only taught the meditation a couple of times a year, so while waiting I went on reading the book and conducting sessions for me and my followers.

While conducting a group session one night, something quite remarkable happened. As I was getting ready to start calling the names of the loved ones, the soft disembodied voice of a man with an Indian accent said, "Paramahansa." I absolutely couldn't believe it. Again I listened while reviewing the session and there it was, clear as day. I was able to find a clip online of Guruji saying his name and, sure enough, it was almost identical to the voice I captured on video. While that response was being spoken, a beautiful slow-moving orb circled around me. This blew my mind, and there was no doubt that Yogananda had visited me and made himself known. It was such an amazing gift and confirmation that yes, even after death, the Guru can still be your teacher.

Shortly after that wonderful occurrence, I was doing a live stream with my followers on YouTube and decided to pull out my DR60 voice recorder and ask a few questions. What I captured, everyone on the live got to witness as it was another miraculous occurrence. On the recorder was a perfect, clear response again saying the name Paramahansa. As my face immediately changed right on camera to shock, I asked for validation if indeed it was the Yogi himself. I then recorded the response "I love it... Josh." I was so emotional I had to end the live stream. Both of these were undeniable occurrences.

The day finally came for me to drive hours down to Miami and learn the Kriya meditation. When I arrived, I entered the meditation hall, and there on the wall hung portraits of each Master, including Jesus and Krishna. For hours, we learned the first four parts of Kriya, took a break for an all-vegetarian meal, and then went back into the hall to learn the other four parts. It was a lot for me to learn and like any good student, I took notes. Afterward, I thanked the monastics and drove back home to where I put my fragmented notes together and studied the meditation practice some more. When I finally felt ready, I practiced my first actual Kriya Yoga meditation. At the end of the hour, I placed my hands over my eyes to perceive light through my third eye and this archway appeared in great detail.

That vision was one of the most vivid I had ever seen in a meditation, and I had to immediately draw what it was I had witnessed. Yogananda writes in another of his books, *The Yoga of Jesus,*

> *"By the right method of meditation and devotion, with the eyes closed and concentrated on the spiritual eye, the devotee knocks at the gates of heaven… a light begins to form in the forehead… it is more difficult for the devotee to go into that light. But by practice of the higher methods, such as Kriya Yoga, the consciousness is led inside the spiritual eye, into another world of vaster dimensions."*[52]

---

[52] From *The Yoga of Jesus,* pages 36 & 37.

It was clear through the intuitive guidance I was receiving and the evidence I was capturing that not only was I led to Kriya Yoga, the holy science of communicating with God, but that my actual Guru Paramahansa Yogananda was very much interacting with me. You can see the captivating story unfold in this powerful video.[53]

As I continued to practice Kriya on a daily basis, I started receiving more in meditation from Jesus. There was no doubt that the Kriya Yoga was expanding my consciousness as I was let in on more about my past. Perhaps I will save that for another book but the visions were powerful. This new daily spiritual practice was certainly bringing me closer to Christ as I felt that I was being Divinely guided even more.

All Paramahansa Yogananda wanted to do was help people connect with their Source, but not just through what was told to them, rather through real experiences. This made sense to me being that was the only way I've come to know God. He confirmed we are the same in death as we were in life unless we change while being alive. This also made sense to me as it showed why the Twelve Steps were so important and why spirits that didn't change while in a body were sometimes stuck. Guruji spoke of the light we receive from God that enters us. This definitely made sense to me as spirits are always talking about the light, not to mention capturing true orbs on camera.

Many of the stories Yogananda shares in his book are so wild and outrageous, a new seeker might not know what to think. But reading these accounts, some by people he knew and some by his own eyewitness, you can't help but start to see the truth in all he's sharing. From the moment I picked up the book, I was hooked.

[53] Watch this powerful video of me being led to Kriya Yoga at HOPEparanormal.com/video Video #31.

Every word on each page truly touched me, and I wasn't the only one. Well over four million copies have been sold, and it has been translated into forty languages. He was the first prominent Indian to be hosted by a US President at the White House and was put on a commemorative stamp by the Indian government. He was beloved by many. In fact, George Harrison of the Beatles kept copies of Yogananda's book to give out as gifts because of how important he felt the book was. George once stated he wouldn't want to live life without it. On the cover of the Beatles' Sargent Pepper Lonely Hearts album, there are many faces but inconspicuously placed are the four Gurus: Swami Sri Yukteswar, Muhavatar Babaji, Lahiri Mahasaya, and Paramahansa Yogananda. As a young teenager, Steve Jobs read the book and it affected him so greatly, he read it every year thereafter. Before his funeral, he pre-purchased five hundred copies to make sure that everyone that attended received one before leaving.

There's a reason these people and millions of others felt this way about the book. It's because it holds the truth. All of these people felt it without seeing pictures or videos as proof. He shared his experiences as a testimony in hopes that each reader would begin seeking for themselves so that they too may experience the same joys of communion with the Divine Creator. One of the very first things we see when opening the book, under the title, is the bible verse John 4:48 NIV, which reads:

> *"Unless you people see miraculous signs and wonders,"*
> *Jesus said, "you will never believe."*

This is why he shares all of his experiences with us and why I am sharing all my experiences with you. We are all meant to have our own that help us transcend barriers and liberate the soul. Sometimes it's the testimony of others that truly helps us in our journey.

When Guruji left his physical body on March 7th, 1952, in Los Angeles, he did so on his own terms. He entered into *Mahasamadhi*, which is a yogi's final conscious exit from the body. He was at a banquet hall full of people giving a speech honoring the Ambassador of India, H. E. Binay R. Sen. After the speech he read a few lines from a poem and turned his eyes upward and collapsed. Days before, he had been hinting to his disciples that he was planning on leaving the world.

In the weeks after his death, his body still showed no signs of any decay or corruptibility. Mr. Harry T. Rowe, Los Angeles Mortuary Director at Forrest Lawn Memorial-Park had this to say about Paramahansa's body, "The absence of any visual signs of decay in the dead body of Paramahansa Yogananda offers the most extraordinary case in our experience... No physical disintegration was visible in his body even twenty days after death... No indication of mold was visible on his skin, and no visible desiccation took place in the body tissues. This state of perfect preservation of a body is, so far as we know from mortuary annals, an unparalleled one... Yogananda's body was apparently in a phenomenal state of immutability."[54]

I can tell you from personal experience he is very much alive and so are the other Masters. I am forever grateful for his guidance and love. He showed me he is very real and cares about helping from the other side just as much as he did when he was here on earth.[55]

Just the other day I heard "ask for Babaji" through the box. While deep in meditation afterward, I saw a vision of Babaji's

---

[54] From *Metaphysical Meditations*, pages 119 & 120.
[55] Watch another powerful video where I contact my Guru at HOPEparanormal.com/video Video #32.

face. Maybe he's letting me know I'm getting closer to being ready. For what, I don't know. Either way, what I do know is that we have Divine Beings wanting very much to help us and when we ask them, They do so. What an absolute blessing that is.

THE IMPORTANCE
OF THIS WORK

THERE'S NO QUESTION FOR ME that this type of work and research is important to human evolution. In a day and age where the world continues to move in the direction of being more and more dependent on technology, society becomes less spiritually conscious. We are now at a point where AI (Artificial Intelligence) is playing a bigger role in the lives of human beings, and I suspect it will only increase. With all the distractions we have now, it makes it harder and harder to quiet the mind and go within ourselves for intuitive self-reflection. With all the apps, social media platforms, streaming platforms, and agendas pushed on to us, it's amazing we get any sleep. Most people have their phones glued to their faces looking for the next five-second clip to satisfy their diminishing attention span. The more this happens, the further society gets away from true spirituality.

On top of that big issue, people just don't know what to believe anymore, and because of that, they close their minds off and stick with what they think they know. We are meant to expand our horizons, grow, and strive for purpose and connection. It's important to understand this physical world is not all there is; in fact, it's just a small fraction of reality. When this is understood through personal spiritual experiences with a Higher Power, we begin seeing a bigger picture. That's what seeing this evidence does for some people. It unlocks a deeper level of understanding for them, a level they already had access to but needed unlocking. It's like one of those optical illusions where it asks you what you see. Once you give an answer to what you think you see, you're shown another image within that main image, and what was nearly invisible moments before is now something you can't unsee. This type of work may not be for the masses to participate in, but it's definitely something that everyone could benefit from by seeing.

In the last part of this book, I'm going to share with you why being called crazy, being attacked by haters, working long hours on videos, and making very little money doing it has all been worth it.

ALL OF THE PEOPLE IT HAS HELPED

In the earlier part of this book, I shared the details of my dark past, the troubles I had seen, and what I needed to do to get out of them. The truth is I have been saved from a life, or even afterlife of hell, and for that, I will continue to work on being a humble servant of the Lord. If I never did another session again or posted another video, I would at least know there were many that have received help from seeing this work. Before I discuss the close group of people to whom I've had the pleasure of bringing forth messages from their deceased loved ones, here are just a few of the comments from followers that have been deeply affected positively by this work.

When people first find me, I love it when they share their initial feeling of what they're seeing and how it has touched them.

> *"I found you a couple of months ago when I first lost my stepmom in February and this channel gave me hope that one day I will be able to talk with her again."*
> *Savannah*

"I've been watching for a while now. I get what you're doing. I can honestly say your research has helped my journey in life." Lisa

"Bless your heart, Josh! Thank you truly for helping to give these amazing souls a voice. I've talked to many people that watch your videos, and it's because of your ability to be sincere and genuine, that these messages find their way through to so many. That's what makes the difference." Amy

Then there are people who were suicidal and seeing these videos has helped to change their mindset. Here in these comments below, the followers that I left anonymous, mention a spirit, Chris, that I helped, who committed suicide. A very powerful set of videos.[56]

"Watching this honestly just changed the way I look at life. I have been suicidal once in my life, but I'm in a good place now and I expect to never feel so low again. But if I do, I'll remember Chris and the others. I don't feel like being in the spirit world alone." Anonymous 1

"I have been very suicidal and I find distraction from that through your videos. You have saved a lot of lives." Anonymous 2

People that have watched me for years continue to appreciate the communication I receive and share with me what it means to them.

---

[56] Watch videos where I deal with suicide, at HOPEparanormal.com/video Videos #33 & 34.

"How powerful and eye-opening. I have tears in my eyes every time I watch your videos. What you do with your gift is so amazing and thoughtful. We need more people in the world like you. Such a blessing." Tina

"I have watched you and others for years and this is probably the best evidence I have ever seen. The DR60 is amazing. You are asking some fantastic questions. I hope that you will continue to ask so that all of us can continue to learn." Carl

"Josh... Please keep up this important work... Not only do you do what I think is so beautiful which is to help lost souls find God but here on this side you do the same. Keep opening people's eyes to the truth, to the light and love. Bringing us all closer to God. Always much appreciation and love." Coni

The comments and messages I receive are so very important and show just how meaningful the sessions are to people. I show you these comments not to brag or build myself up but to show how a Power greater than myself is working through me, including many others doing this kind of work. Yes, I get a wonderful personal feeling when I receive comments like the ones I'm showing you, but I get more satisfaction knowing that God is using me to help His children. I don't know that there could be a greater feeling, in my opinion. When I read these comments, I want to cry. Not only does it mean God is helping those people, who are searching for hope, but that he took me, someone who was wasting his life hurting people, and transformed me. He transformed me into someone He could use to help others. He took a floundering existence and gave it true purpose. As I write this, tears are literally falling down my face. I don't think I could ever express the gratitude that I have.

A SPECIAL GROUP

In 2018, shortly before the birth of my second daughter, Emersyn, who by the way was born on Halloween, I decided to start a group online that would serve as another catalyst for better spirit communication. This group of people known as patrons were true followers of my work and wanted to know more about what I was doing. Many of them were looking to reach a deceased loved one but, in addition, wanted to understand more about what I had learned over the years. Being that it was a monthly membership, for the price of two cups of coffee, patrons were able to submit a deceased loved one's name each month for a group session I conducted. Once a month, I asked for up to 100 people in each session, sometimes receiving close to 45 validating responses. In addition to the group sessions, I did live streams discussing different topics, I taught a multitude of intuitive classes, and shared some of my most intimate moments from doing this work.

Quickly, each one of these people became beloved members of my soul family. Not only were my connections deepening with each member of the group, but real friendships were being formed amongst the other members. After several months, more people kept joining, and the patrons that had been there from the beginning went out of their way to greet the new members and make them feel welcome. It was such an amazing thing to watch.

At the same time, the communication with the guides and the members' deceased loved ones got better. During the live streams, Michael and the other guides were coming through with amazing messages. During the group sessions, the patrons' loved ones were giving detailed information about the other side and answering questions with specific information. It was absolutely amazing.

Because I was reaching out to some of the same deceased loved ones each month, that allowed me to form beautiful connections with some of them. Coming through month after month with clear, relevant messages, the patrons started to really understand their loved ones were far from dead. There have been so many powerful stories I could write a whole other book about them, but one worth mentioning would be Natalie and her brother, Renee. Natalie joined the patron group and wanted to speak to her brother but wanted to start out by doing an intuitive reading just using my abilities as a medium to connect. The reading went extremely well with me describing exactly what he looked like, how he died, and whom he was close to. At one point during the reading, he told me he was right next to her. This was something she could feel and confirmed it. For her, there was no doubt it was him.

After it was over, she asked if she could book a private box session where I use my equipment in addition to my intuitive ability. I agreed and we conducted one the following week. During the private session, Renee was able to connect very well and use his own voice to speak as Natalie was able to recognize his tone. Not only was Renee able to use his own voice, but would also do so on multiple devices, directly answering most of Natalie's questions. In the group sessions that came after that private session, Renee was a regular coming through each time extremely strong.[57] He even offered to help deal with Frank, which was wild.

Recently, I have found a way to run the group session using chopped-up, indiscernible voice tracks that don't contain actual words. No radios, no apps, or sound banks of words. This way, I don't have to deal with false positives, and if a word comes

---

[57] Watch a video where I'm reaching people's loved ones, including Renee, Natalie's brother at HOPEparanormal.com/video Video #35.

through, it's undeniably a spirit using it. Since that discovery, the communication has gotten better once again. Coupled with having patrons ask for their loved ones live during the session, it's really improved the results.[58]

I don't know what will happen to the group in the years to come, but, regardless, I've come to know some of the finest people I've ever met. So much of what I've done wouldn't have been possible without them. Even when it came to the book, it would've taken even longer to publish without their help. I've never seen such amazing support in my life. They tell me they're all grateful and blessed to have found me and the work I do, and I beg to differ. It is I who is truly blessed for their presence in my life.

KEEP SEEKING NO MATTER WHAT

Socrates once said, "An unexamined life is not a life worth living." Why did he say that? Because the search for our true selves is the only one that's truly worth it. Of course, it's okay to work hard, have careers, and save money to attain material things, such as a house and car, to enjoy our lives and the wonderful things in it. But not at the cost of forsaking who we really are. These material things we can't take with us to the other side, whether that's next week or in eighty years. If we seek Divine guidance, meditate regularly, live rightly according to God's will, we become liberated. We gain access to a limitless kingdom of omnipresent Spirit. Of course, we must be willing to do the work, though.

"Don't depend on death to liberate you from your imperfections. You are exactly the same after death as you were before. Nothing changes; you only give up

---

[58] Watch a video where I'm reaching loved ones using a new sound source I created at HOPEparanormal.com/video Video #36.

the body. If you are a thief or liar or a cheater before death, you don't become an angel merely by dying. If such were possible, then let us all go and jump in the ocean now and become angels at once! Whatever you have made of yourself thus far, so will you be hereafter. And when you reincarnate, you will bring the same nature with you. To change, you have to make the effort. This world is the place to do it."

Paramahansa Yogananda

After being at the lowest place in my life, addicted to drugs and alcohol, a violent offender, who served multiple years behind bars and then became a successful but controversial entrepreneur, the last thing I ever pictured myself doing was speaking to Jesus and helping spirits through radios and recorders. If it was up to me, I would've chosen to continue building up my assets and measuring my success by what I was able to accumulate materially. But instead, I began evaluating my progress in life by looking at my spiritual and internal growth.

What I began to see was how that glaring weakness, my sensitive nature that I had worked so hard to get rid of, was proving to be my greatest strength. In a way, I had come full circle, but it seemed I had to go through a form of hell to get there. A baptism by fire. It made me think of a quote the brilliant comedian Dave Chappelle shared while accepting an award. His mom used to tell him, "Sometimes you gotta be a lion so you can be the lamb you really are." Well, I'm still in the process of becoming that lamb, and I know I have a way to go, but I'm on the path. That's important. The person I am today is a far cry from who I used to be when I first embarked on this wild journey. If someone like me was able to recover from such a seemingly hopeless state of mind, then anyone can. The best part? We just have to try. All who persist with true sincerity will enter the kingdom of God in this life.

> *"Ask and it will be given to you; seek and you will find; knock and the door will be opened to you. For everyone who asks receives; he who seeks finds; and to him who knocks, the door will be opened."*
> *Jesus's words– Matthew 7:7–8 NIV*

In sending love and light to all the sincere seekers who have embarked on the spiritual journey of Self-Realization, it is my **hope** that each soul breaks their karmic bonds and ascends to the highest heavenly level.

May the Father of Light always guide the way!

Printed in the United States
By Bookmasters